Accompaniment, Community and Nature

of related interest

Migration and Faith Communities
Edited by Lia Shimada
ISBN 978 1 78592 387 6
eISBN 978 1 78450 745 9

The Role of Religion in Peacebuilding
Crossing the Boundaries of Prejudice and Distrust
Edited by Pauline Kollontai, Sue Yore and Sebastian Kim
ISBN 978 1 78592 336 4
eISBN 978 1 78450 657 5

Loving Your Neighbour in an Age of Religious Conflict
A New Agenda for Interfaith Relations
James Walters
ISBN 978 1 78592 563 4
eISBN 978 1 78450 961 3

Learning to Live Well Together
Case Studies in Interfaith Diversity
Tom Wilson and Riaz Ravat
ISBN 978 1 78592 194 0
eISBN 978 1 78450 467 0

Fortress Britain?
Ethical approaches to immigration policy for a post-Brexit Britain
Edited by Ben Ryan
ISBN 978 1 78592 309 8
eISBN 978 1 78450 620 9

ACCOMPANIMENT, COMMUNITY AND NATURE

Overcoming Isolation, Marginalisation and Alienation Through Meaningful Connection

JONATHAN HERBERT

Jessica Kingsley Publishers
London and Philadelphia

Material from the *Tao Te Ching* (Palmer 1993) is reproduced with kind permission from Martin Palmer and in memory of his co-author Jay Ramsay who died on 30 December 2018.

Scripture quotations are from New Revised Standard Version Bible: Anglicized Edition, copyright © 1989, 1995 National Council of the Churches of Christ in the United States of America. Used by permission. All rights reserved.

First published in 2020
by Jessica Kingsley Publishers
73 Collier Street
London N1 9BE, UK
and
400 Market Street, Suite 400
Philadelphia, PA 19106, USA

www.jkp.com

Copyright © Jonathan Herbert 2020

Library of Congress Cataloging in Publication Data
A CIP catalog record for this book is available from the Library of Congress

British Library Cataloguing in Publication Data
A CIP catalogue record for this book is available from the British Library

ISBN 978 1 78592 547 4
eISBN 978 1 78450 945 3

Printed and bound in Great Britain

For Brother Kentigern John
of the Society of St Francis

Contents

Acknowledgements

To all those over the years who have accompanied me, with particular thanks for those who have so patiently and skilfully encouraged me and inspired my inner journey: Melvyn Matthews, Will Thompson, Graham Chadwick, Sister Gemma, Sister Mairead, Sue Langdon.

For those organisations that have taught me how to be alongside others and continue to imbue me with vision and hope: the Simon Community, L'Arche, Citizens, Christian International Peace Services, the Ecumenical Accompaniment Programme in Palestine and Israel, the Churches Network for Gypsies, Travellers and Roma.

The Pilsdon Community, and the hundreds of people I lived with there, continue to be formative in how I try and live with others, as does Hilfield Friary Community, which continues to teach me about our interconnectedness with the earth, our common home. Thanks to the brothers and community members there for giving me the space to write. To the Society of St Francis for giving me time to write in the apartment in Assisi, and, similarly, Shirley Edwards for her cottage in the Lake District.

I'm grateful to Betty Smith Billington, Sylvia Harrison, Roger Redding, Michael Johnson and many other Travellers for teaching me wisdom from the nomadic way of life.

Thanks to Patrick Woodhouse and Toby Jones for reading and encouraging me with the early draft of the book. Thanks to Ruby Hale for coming up with the idea for the cover design. To Katie

Lange for her insight into the theme of the book and help with the text. To Sara Whitehouse for her photographic skills and Simon Munro for his technical support.

Finally, to Suzi for never letting me take myself too seriously and accompanying me so fearlessly over the years.

Preface

SITTING ON THE STEPS

When I was eight years old, I took on the responsibility for making sandwiches for the numerous homeless people, or tramps as we called them, who came to the door of the vicarage where I lived. I'd cut and butter the bread and make strong dark sweet tea, which I'd take out to the doorstep and then, for some reason, I'd always sit with the men. Sometimes they'd tell me gripping tales of life on the road, sometimes they'd say nothing and I'd just sit companionably with them. This was the beginning of a pattern of learning to accompany others. Later on, I left home and went to live in the Simon Community, working and living with the homeless in North London, a charity that had a greater stress on being with, rather than seeking to rehabilitate or change, people. The idea of learning to be with people rather than always trying to find a solution to their problems stayed with me, as I later went to live in a group home with people with learning difficulties and then to work for the church on a couple of run-down council estates, where what people wanted from me, it seemed, were not bright ideas and solutions to their problems but a simple willingness to share in their lives. A natural progression of this, which has further deepened my understanding of accompaniment, has been to live in community with the many joys and challenges that brings.

Being invited to be part of the World Council of Churches Ecumenical Accompaniment Programme in Palestine and Israel in 2010 allowed me to put a name to this way of being with people and helped me reflect further on accompaniment as a tool for peacemaking, as did the time I was able to spend in an area of conflict in north-east Uganda.

My chaplaincy work with Gypsies and Travellers has taught me to depend on accompaniment as the vital tool for establishing trust and relationships with Travellers, as accompaniment is a skill this community has in abundance. These days, I'm more likely to be sitting next to a campfire than on some stone steps, but the process is the same and accompaniment remains, for me, a powerful way of breaking down the loneliness, exclusion and polarisation that seems so endemic in the Western world.

INTRODUCTION

I wake to the sound of the alarm on my phone; it's hot and it's dark in the windowless room I've been sleeping in. I pull on my clothes, fold up the blanket and tiptoe down the hall, trying not to wake the sleeping household of Francis, his wife and their five children, and the five orphans from his brother's family who they care for. I've stayed overnight with them in Iriri, a rough market town in the poorest, dustiest part of eastern Uganda called Karamoja, in order to catch the bus to the capital, Kampala. No one can be quite sure when the bus is going to arrive, as it will only set off from its base in Moroto when there are enough passengers aboard. I need to be at the stop by 4 a.m. just in case it comes early, as there's only one bus a day. I pull on my backpack and, as I go to unlock the door, Francis appears, trying to shake the tiredness out of his body. I assume he's up to say goodbye and relock the door, but instead he comes outside into the pitch darkness and says he'll accompany me to the bus stop. I'm glad of his companionship as immediately dogs start barking, and I realise I'd struggle to find the way. He leads me through the compound, past mud huts with grass thatch, the walls so thin you can hear the occupants snoring, past blockwork shacks with tin roofs and onto the main dirt track, which serves as the high street. I turn to thank him again and say goodbye, but he insists on staying with me. I try to persuade him to go back to bed but he stays. We don't say much, just look up at the dark mass of the huge hill overshadowing the town and listen to a couple of drunks still drinking, talking nonsense in the shopfront behind us. We sit together companionably enough and wait and wait, and eventually, just as it's beginning to grow lighter, we hear the growl of the bus engine. I climb aboard and thank him for his hospitality, but most of all for being with me in the dark hours before the dawn.

Those couple of hours are what I would describe as accompaniment, a way of being with others which has somehow become lost in our culture, a culture that stresses the need for independence and personal autonomy. In rural Uganda, it's just part of daily life and a totally natural way of supporting and enjoying other people and a simple expression of how people belong together. Sitting on the bench with Francis, I thanked him for being with me, and I introduced the idea of accompaniment to him; he just laughed at me and said, 'But that's what everyone does around here,' then quoted an African proverb to me: 'Don't walk behind me or you'll make me feel too self-important and puffed up, don't walk in front of me lest you leave me behind, rather walk alongside me and we'll face life joyfully together.'

I was glad to be accompanied by Francis. It helped me feel safe that morning, it took away the fear that can come with loneliness, but more importantly it made me feel like I'd received that most precious gift of all, somebody else's time. He was happy to sit and wait, doing nothing, expecting nothing, which is such a contrast to the way I've been programmed – to be aware of time and the need to get things done. In the West, time is seen as something lineal that's going to run out, so we need to make the best use of it, pack as much as we can into this one life. My encounters with people in rural Africa, India and the Pacific, with Gypsies and Travellers, and with those of a more spiritual bent, have led me to understand time as something more cyclical and something to be shared. Accompaniment is a process that has at its heart this giving of time to another, not expecting instant outcomes, but rather to see the act of being fully present with another as something that can bring joy and comfort to the accompanier and those accompanied.

Could accompaniment just be friendship by another name? I've often asked myself this, and it certainly bears many of the marks of good friendship, but I would argue it's less than friendship and also much more. After I got on that bus, I never saw Francis again, so had no real time to build a friendship I know I would have valued, but his sitting waiting with me, though fleeting, still represented something significant for me, leaving me with a deep sense of gratitude. Of course, good accompaniment has led me into deep friendships, but I've also accompanied others I don't like, find difficult and would never call my friends. I've learnt to live well with people who have such different world views from me, and personalities I would naturally shy away from; and because of what I have learnt about ways of accompanying, most keenly through living in community with very different people, I'd say that such people have given me many gifts of self-understanding. Like Francis being prepared to sit on that bench with me, I've learnt to sit with and acknowledge some of the uncomfortable feelings some people provoke in me. By sitting with rather than ignoring or repressing these feelings I've usually been able to grow in compassion for those people I find difficult and certainly for myself. That still doesn't mean I like them, but it helps me live well with them.

Could accompaniment also be something akin to counselling? Well, it bears some traits of a therapeutic relationship, good listening and commitment to the other, but it's probably not so tightly boundaried as the counsellor–client relationship. It can happen anywhere and any time of day, as I found with Francis. There's not necessarily a beginning and an end, and it's often more mutual and less likely to create dependence; rather it seeks to build interdependence. The accompanier, like the counsellor, is helped by an attitude of humility, of not thinking you know what the other is thinking, feeling or what might be good for them, not judging. Unlike most of the short-term counselling now offered by the National Health Service, it is prepared to give time to the other, to allow change to happen in its own mysterious way, and not be time driven. Accompaniment isn't just between individuals. I would argue that you can accompany a community, a group of people, as I do in my role as chaplain to Gypsies and Travellers, or even two peoples, as the Ecumenical Accompaniment Programme in Palestine and Israel seeks to do.

Francis' life was so different to mine, yet he was able to accompany me, and accompaniment is a tool for crossing apparent divides between people, and a way of building bridges. He told me that morning that, apart from playing football, which was his great love, being prepared to journey with those who were different was the best way to break down barriers between people. He was a man who didn't mind taking risks, having moved to Iriri to set up a church ten years earlier, when it was wild and lawless. Breaking down barriers entails risk, daring to be open to meet someone who appears to be very different, and seeking to understand and walk a little way in the shoes of the other, which inevitably leads to the understanding that they're not so different after all.

Accompaniment offers a way to build trust between people, as it's not a process that demands quick answers or has a particular predetermined end in mind. Learning to be present with a person without needing to use words is something a lot of people fear in a world so full of often superficial and unlimited communication. Working alongside someone without the need to comment, justify or control what's going on might be something for us to relearn in our task-orientated and time-driven culture. The afternoon previous to our dawn vigil at the bus stop, after we'd first met, Francis had taken me to watch a local football game, then we'd played pool for an hour in the local bar before going back to meet his family and share food. We didn't say much to each other, just enjoyed that time together. He didn't want anything from me, he just seemed to want to share time with me, and that's how trust and all good relationships can grow.

In the peacemaking work I was involved with in that part of Uganda, and in the work I do between the settled community and Travellers in the UK, it's the building of trust that breaks down fear and division. This slow building of trust through accompanying others is something that is usually hidden, not trumpeted or put on public display, which of course could undermine it. Much of the process of accompaniment can seem mundane and goes on unheralded, but it is a vital building block in the establishment of just and peaceable communities. It's as much an intuitive skill as a learnt behaviour, and for it to be effective and affective it can't be too formalised. Like any interpersonal process, it can be abused, but because of its fairly simple application, it's a highly accessible way of developing and restoring right relationships on a micro and a macro level. A key part of accompanying well is to learn how to prevent our own wounded sense of self-importance getting in the way of those we walk alongside. It's not about pushing our own agenda, but allowing space for the other to find their sense of belonging. Often many organisations become cut off from people and remote because they fail to make time to use the simple tool of accompaniment.

At heart, it's a way of learning to live well with otherness and difference, whilst reminding us that we all belong together, and can draw us out of the dangers of inward-looking individualism. Accompaniment is never dismissive of others; through being with others who are very different, it's a form of encounter that can encourage others and ourselves to shift our perceptions and change our world view. It's not something that's passive, though, and it requires us to summon up the courage to walk with those who are very different and would wish to be in opposition to us. Accompanying a people might lead us to taking sides, particularly with an oppressed and vilified group such as Gypsies and Travellers, but, vitally, it never seeks to close off the possibility of communication with those who take opposing views to us. It offers the possibility, as Gandhi famously put it, to be the change, and be the change alongside others.

If we extend it to our relationship with the natural world, then it offers a way of repairing the breach between ourselves and the planet we are wounding, largely through our objectification of it. By drawing us into relationship with others, including all forms of life, accompaniment challenges the notion that the natural world is something to be constantly raided for resources to maintain a deeply toxic and unsustainable way of life. By walking alongside nature, a process of re-enchantment can happen, which is far more likely to spur us to work towards a sustainable future than dire warnings (true as they are) about the consequences of climate change.

If it's loneliness, polarisation and fear of the other that are at the centre of our deep unease as individuals and societies, then a rediscovery of accompaniment will be a vital part of repairing the torn fabric of our world. It's a process that's dynamic, comforting, challenging, painful and often joyful. The phrase 'walking alongside', as well as reflecting the idea of being with, also suggests movement, a journey. As I bade farewell to Francis and stepped onto that bus, just as dawn was coming to Iriri, I knew I was at the beginning of a journey to Kampala; what follows in this book is a description of my journey of learning about and examining the practice of accompaniment.

1

ALIENATION

It's early spring and, for once, I'm lost in the moment, enjoying the natural rhythm of forking over the earth in the large sheltered vegetable garden of the Pilsdon Community. I notice the birds singing, the sound of the wind rustling the new leaves on the mighty ash tree on the edge of the plot. 'What a place just to be,' I'm thinking. Suddenly, there's the sound of loud angry shouting, and I feel that familiar sense of visceral dread deep in my guts. I want to run away, ignore the conflict, but instead, still holding my garden fork, I run towards it. I race into the farmyard at the back of Pilsdon Manor and there, in the corner of the yard clinging to the gatepost, is Max; clamped to his legs are two strangers, trying to rip him off the post and bundle him into their getaway car, which the driver is revving up. All the sound and fury is coming from Rachel, usually a very quiet, withdrawn young woman, who is raging and ranting at them with a pent-up fury and force that is shaking her body. As Darren, a burly Sudanese man, also enters the fray, the kidnappers let go, dive into the car and screech off.

Max is shaking, Rachel is shaking, I'm shaking, but Darren just stands there smiling with a huge grin and says, 'I don't think they were your friends, were they Max?'

The whole scene could have been taken from an action film and was over in seconds, but, in many ways, it contained a number of the themes I want to think about throughout the journey of this book. Packed into the drama of those few seconds were fear, rage, addiction, alienation, violence, need, desperation, courage, risk and generosity.

Max had been seeking sanctuary at the Pilsdon Community, a place of refuge for people recovering from addiction, mental breakdown, homelessness and many other vicissitudes of life. He had been a drug dealer in nearby Bridport and, in exchange for giving witness testimony in court against some of the main players in the drug trade in south-west England, he had been offered a new identity and immunity from prosecution by the police. Whilst he was waiting for this to come through, we had offered him a place to hide in our remote rural community, in what we wrongly assumed would be a safe house. He himself was struggling to break free of an addiction to cannabis and, like so many at Pilsdon, his clinging on to that gatepost was how many would describe the reality of their own battles to stay off alcohol or drugs.

Rachel was a young Eastern European who'd been trafficked and forced into prostitution, but had escaped and was beginning to rebuild her life at Pilsdon. She said she was just walking past when she saw the thugs attacking Max, and she knew she couldn't take them on physically so channelled all her rage at her former captors into an extended rant at the kidnappers. The force of her rage, an outpouring of hot anger against the violence committed against her, had echoed round the farmyard and had saved Max by nonplussing the kidnappers and summoning help. Later, Rachel was able to say to me, 'That's how angry I am about what happened to me. My anger's as loud as the sound of my shouts echoing round that yard. I was terrified, but I couldn't stand by and see someone else be violated. Somehow my fear gave me courage.'

Darren was an asylum seeker we had freed from Pentonville prison by posting bail for him whilst he awaited his asylum application. As a young Dinka tribesman, he'd been a cattle herder in South Sudan and then a soldier in the Sudanese People's Liberation Army. He'd been captured, taken to the north of the country, escaped from prison, crossed the Sahara Desert, worked in Libya to save money, to then be smuggled across Europe to the UK. He'd suffered much and, like Rachel, was struggling with depression. He was a big man, built like a heavyweight boxer, with something of the warrior about him, and as he burst onto the scene, followed by me with a garden fork in hand, the assailants fled. They must have been surprised to have been met with such resistance in what the Pilsdon Community, in its publicity, described as 'a quiet place of refuge and healing'.

Max was moved on that day and a successful prosecution went ahead, but this incident highlighted to me much about the sense of alienation so prevalent in Western society, a society that is addictive and highly individualistic, where so many live with such a strong sense of loneliness and isolation that they feel they are only just clinging on. Max was seen not as a person, but a problem to be fixed or eliminated, to allow the supply of drugs, with its associated profits, to continue. Rachel's rage too spoke in a wider sense of the terrible cost when men, women and children are objectified and seen as commodities to be bought and sold and used or abused. Darren, the asylum seeker and rescuer, speaks to me of how much our society will be enriched when, instead of rejecting and 'othering' those fleeing places of war and death, we build a narrative of acceptance and generosity, and learn to welcome difference and the skills and energy so many migrants bring. Lastly, the garden fork I was wielding is a sign of the need for us to stop ignoring the suffering of our planet and seeing it as a resource to be plundered, but rather to see it as a source of life and our common home.

My journey through this book is about first seeing the danger and threats we face, the crisis of loneliness and alienation we are living in, acknowledging the damage that has been done by the destructive forces of individualistic thinking, and then journeying towards a more holistic understanding of what it means to live well together. On the way, I shall look at ways of countering alienation, places of refuge, how we learn to be with one another, how to resist the temptation of easy and divisive answers and how we might find a sense of being truly at home with ourselves and each other. Central to this journey of discovery will be an attempt to answer the questions of why we have become so lonely and alienated from one another and how to re-enchant our relationships with ourselves, others and the earth, with a renewed sense of kinship and connectedness. Put more simply, how do we learn to live more generously? The notion that has helped me explore many of these questions has been the practice of accompaniment, and I offer it as a simple but effective tool in countering alienation and leading us to a renewed sense of belonging.

If accompaniment is a relatively simple process that can do much to build up individuals and community life and bring joy into our relationships with one another, then why do we so seldom encounter it? What is it within us that resists living in this way? Our failure to risk accompanying others, I will argue, is because Western society has become so dominated by the story of separation, which leads to the thinking that being alienated from one another is the natural state of affairs. Alienation has many causes but if we can name them, then it may be possible to come up with the more positive narrative that we do indeed belong together. My opening story illustrated some of the roots of alienation, which I would describe as objectification, exclusion and disconnection.

OBJECTIFICATION

If you were looking for an example of alienation and the breakdown of trust, all brought about by objectification, then being a victim, like Rachel, of sexual abuse and the feelings of betrayal, fear, anger, guilt and shame provoked by the abusers has to be one of the darkest places victims are forced to inhabit. Survivors have told me that, unless supported by skilled and sustained therapeutic support, the legacy of their abuse can very quickly lead to depression and sometimes suicide.

As a young priest, I accompanied a family through the revelation of abuse, prosecution of the perpetrator and their struggles to survive its impact. It was the late 1980s, before safeguarding had begun to be practised by the Anglican Church, when the younger of two brothers aged 16 and 18 who came to the church youth club disclosed to me that, for the last six years, he and his brother had been regularly raped and sexually abused by one of my predecessors who had been a trainee priest in the parish. The man still lived locally, and would invite the two young men to stay over with him on the pretext that he was giving the parents a break, as they had three other children to care for. The day after David, the younger brother, had found the strength to tell me he wished it to stop, the man was due to come and take them away again. I told him how courageous he had been and that I needed to tell the bishop, suggested he tell his parents, and also told him that the police were likely to be involved. I promised him that I would support him and his brother as much as I could through what was likely to be a long and difficult process.

That night he told his parents, and the following evening, when their abuser visited, the young men pretended to be ill so that they wouldn't have to go to his house. Their father later told me that he always knew something was wrong with his older sons but could never work it out, but now it all made sense. That evening, he offered the priest a large glass of his favourite whisky, laced with enough of his crushed-up heart pills to kill him and avenge the abuse of his sons. Fortunately, the priest refused the drink, put out that the young men weren't coming with him.

I was summoned to see the bishop, who in a spirit of openness not always adhered to in those times, agreed that we should involve the police, commenting about the negative publicity to the church with a cricket analogy: 'We'll just have to bat this one out.' I agreed to accompany the young men through the whole process.

I went with them to a harrowing three-hour interview with two detectives who worked through the catalogue of abuse in graphic detail. It was intensely painful for the younger brother, who had a deep sense of shame and violation, but the elder brother seemed to have normalised his abuse and said things like 'We did the usual thing.' Reflecting later, I found this more disturbing than the younger brother's tears and numbness in giving explicit detail.

Once we'd completed the police interviews, I decided to take the two brothers away to avoid the inevitable publicity and potential press intrusion. I managed to book them in for two weeks at the Pilsdon Community, that hidden rural place of safety I described earlier. Here, the brothers met Ron, a survivor of childhood abuse, who was an enormous help and support and gave them hope for the future.

The next obstacle for the brothers to overcome was the trial at the Crown Court. Their abuser was pleading not guilty in the hope that the boys would be intimidated by the thought of a court appearance. They found the courage to go, and I sat next to them in court and watched their abuser change his plea to guilty as soon as he saw them, knowing the strength of the evidence against him. A senior clergyman was called to give a character witness in mitigation for the defendant and enraged the family by saying in archaic language that 'He was a man that gave into the temptations of the flesh.' 'What, am I then just a piece of meat?' the younger brother asked. That was probably how the perpetrator saw him, as little more than a body to be abused, and it's this objectification of people that the porn and sex industry thrives on. People like Rachel aren't seen as fellow human beings but rather as objects to be bought and sold.

The Time's Up movement, sparked by the accusations of many women describing film producer Harvey Weinstein as a serial sexual abuser, is a ray of hope in the hidden world of the sexual exploitation of others, but also revealed the extent of manipulation and abuse men with power have managed to get away with. The challenge to objectification, particularly of women's bodies, has a long way to go if we are to build a healthier and safer world. In a 2017 episode of the UK political satire show *Have I Got News for You*, Ian Hislop, one of the two male lead presenters, commented on the recent parliamentary scandal surrounding sexual harassment of women working there as fairly negligible in the wider scheme of injustice around the world. He was quickly put down, though, by comedienne and political activist Jo Brand, chairing the show, who said, 'What you don't realise, Ian, is how exhausting it is for 50 per cent of the population to have the continual drip, drip, drip of harassment and objectification.'

The objectification of the human body can lead to human trafficking, in which people like Rachel are smuggled in as goods to be traded and used, seen as mere commodities and sold to the highest bidder. It's the same philosophy that has justified slavery throughout history. It was also used to justify the trivialisation of 'native life' in the British Colonies. This objectification of people reached its height in the apartheid years in South Africa, 'apartheid' being an Afrikaans word for separate development.

Apartheid is no more in South Africa, but the desire for clear racial divisions and separateness still has its appeal to many in the UK. The strong focus by those in favour of Brexit in the 2016 referendum campaign on people's fear of immigration, and the success of appealing to the public with images suggesting the country was being overrun by refugees, appealed to many poor, alienated, white working-class voters feeling marginalised by the establishment. UKIP infamously unveiled huge advertising hoardings with pictures of large numbers of Syrian refugees with the words 'the country is at breaking point'. People responded to this narrative that we have limited resources that will be used up by migrants from distant lands, who will take over our schools and overwhelm 'our' National Health Service. What didn't occur to many was that our National Health Service is only kept going because of the contribution of tens of thousands of doctors, nurses and cleaners, from the European Union and other parts of the world. The whole way the debate was framed was to see immigrants from Europe, the Middle East and Africa as 'other' and a threat to British jobs, housing, education and access to the National Health Service. The promotion of xenophobia to win a debate and division as a tool to win political support have dangerous precedents in Europe.

On the night of 14 June 2017, the fire at Grenfell Tower in North Kensington, one of the wealthiest boroughs in England, brought into the spotlight the huge inequalities and neglect of immigrant communities in Britain. Housed in Grenfell Tower were refugees from Eritrea, Sudan, Somalia, Syria and Afghanistan, and black descendants of migrant workers from the Caribbean in the 1950s. I wondered whether Darren had ended up there, as I knew he had gone to London but lost touch with him once he'd gained the right to stay here. I went through the names of the 71 who died there and he wasn't one, but it was just the sort of place I'd expect him to be living. Visiting the scene some months afterwards, I was struck by the similarity of the burnt-out block and pictures of places such as Aleppo and Homs from the war in Syria. Paul Salgado, a local community worker, writing about the fire, echoes my thoughts:

> The countries they came from to find refuge and hope in London are a list of war-torn disasters – Afghanistan, Somalia, Sudan, Eritrea, Colombia, Syria – that have now become one in the war zone, the disaster area, the crime scene, that tower that looms over us, reaper black, silent and unforgiving, with its glassless windows like the empty eye sockets of skulls unearthed from mass graves. (Salgado 2017)

I'm sorry now to have to agree with an Afghan man I met at the 'Jungle', a refugee camp in Calais in France, where refugees were waiting to attempt to cross over into the UK, that Britain is no longer a place of welcome to refugees and those fleeing war violence and intimidation. Instead, they are seen by the government as a threat, a problem. He was the first person I met as I entered the camp and he harangued me, saying, 'You British, you come to our country bombing us and preaching human rights to us. Where are our human rights here! Look at this place! Fuck your country, fuck your human rights.' I stood and I listened to the man's anger and despair, agreeing with most of it, just having to soak up his rage. He walked off first and I was left with a huge sense of despair as I moved further into a camp where so much pain, loss, numbness, fear and anger seemed to coalesce. The only hope people had to cling to was the thought of arriving in London, but, for many, I knew that could lead to another form of destitution and potentially deportation back to where they had struggled so hard to leave.

These days, when people from around the world in some kind of distress contact me about visiting Hilfield Friary, where I live, I'm ashamed to say that I usually discourage them from coming and tell them that Britain is no longer a country that welcomes refugees or people under threat or in danger in their own countries. Britain may have once been a place of safety and opportunity for those fleeing oppression and tyranny, but not any more. I tell people that if you do manage to get into the country, you may quickly find yourself with no recourse to public funds or legal protection, and unless you have family, you may well end up destitute on the streets or in an immigration removal centre sited in a former prison, waiting to be deported.

We had a man living at Pilsdon who'd come from a West African country to Britain when he was ten years old with his family who were fleeing political persecution. The family had been granted asylum, but he had never got round to getting a British passport. He was well read, highly articulate, and spoke like a traditional BBC presenter. Isaac had worked in the West End theatres of London and his favourite party piece was to recite John of Gaunt's deathbed prophecy from Shakespeare's *Richard II*. He has also lived here for 40 years, but the Home Office attempted to deport him because he didn't have a British passport and had difficulty tracing his father's passport from 40 years back, in which he was named. He was lucky: the community was able to help fight his case and he had friends who could vouch for him, and we were able to bring influence to bear from somebody the community knew in the House of Lords. So he remains here, but others, with less support yet equally British, who've lived here over 40 years, end up being returned to their country of origin, to which they have no ties, and in fact may be in danger or forced into destitution. This systematic targeting of people without the right papers is all caused by the cynical pursuit of keeping the numbers of immigrants down to satisfy the xenophobic instincts of a toxic and vociferous lobby promoting the false narrative that resources are limited and we need to look after 'our own'. Theresa May, before she became British prime minister, whilst Home Secretary and responsible for those seeking asylum and safety in this country, talked about the need to create 'a hostile environment' for those seeking refugee status and safety at these shores. There's a huge human cost to this and it always seems to be the poorest and most vulnerable who are targeted by the Border Agency and other private firms profiting from the destruction of lives. It's a kind of human trafficking in reverse that only really gains traction because people are objectified as 'other' and leads to much social exclusion.

EXCLUSION

In my work with Gypsies and Travellers, I still feel shock at the extreme levels of hostility and prejudice faced by these much-maligned communities. Trevor Phillips, former chair of the Campaign for Racial Equality, compared the racism today meted out to Gypsies and Travellers as akin to the experience of the black population living in the Deep South of the USA in the 1950s. I visit a council-run site in Salisbury, which reminds me of a post-war bomb site and is in an appalling state of disrepair. The site was built in the early 1970s to provide pitches for nomadic people unable to travel as a result of the forced settlement arising from the 1968 Caravans Act, and no money has been spent on improving the site since. As you enter it, there are huge concrete blocks resembling anti-tank or anti-terrorism defences scattered outside and inside the site to prevent any unauthorised encampments or family members parking up nearby. For years, people have been fly-tipping around the entrance to the site and the council has done little to prevent it. Around all the pitches, the neglected land is overgrown, blocking light and harbouring a huge rat population that has been known to gnaw through electric cables in people's vehicles. Electricity supplies regularly cut out if it rains, and if it rains hard, the blocked storm drains lead to flooding. It reminds me of the Jungle refugee camp outside Calais, yet it's been there for over 40 years. The neglect of the site is symptomatic of a perhaps unwitting institutional racism that ignores the need of an often hidden minority who have an undeserved reputation as being difficult to work with.

Finally the council woke up to the need to do something for its two Salisbury sites but it was unable to raise sufficient funds and find a contractor willing to bring them up to standards stipulated by the Mobile Homes Act, so decided to privatise the sites by selling them off to a private landlord. As one of the Travellers said, 'The council are like Pontius Pilate washing their hands of us.'

I went to the Wiltshire council meeting to agree to the sale of the two Salisbury sites, along with Travellers from both sites, who spoke of their fears that, as in other parts of the country, a private landlord could up the rents to the extent that they would be unable to pay and end up being evicted, and shared dark stories of intimidation by rogue landlords. They also rightly stressed the lack of accountability private landlords have compared to public institutions like the council or housing associations. They were politely listened to, but the decision to privatise went ahead. Worse still, at the same meeting, a proposal to investigate setting up three temporary stopping places for Travellers in different parts of the county was concluded by the county councillor proposing the motion making a joke, saying, 'Let's pray to God none of them end up in one of our divisions.' One of the Travellers in the public gallery turned to me, furious, and said, 'That's racist, you know.' It was, and is symptomatic of the thinking and lack of action that perpetuates the exclusion and alienation of Travellers and many other groups in our society.

It's highly likely that the councillor had never met a Traveller and was basing his speech on negative stereotypes that abound in the media, used to condemn and exclude a whole race of people. This is similar to the austerity narrative where those needing financial assistance are often popularly portrayed as scroungers, although more than half of the social welfare budget in the UK goes to support the state pension. Pensioners, of course, are exempt from public ridicule and cuts, as they are consistently the people most likely to vote.

Public services, since 2010, have been cut to the bare minimum because of an ideology that seeks to reduce the power of the state and promote private wealth. This works well for the top 10 per cent of earners, but the remainder of the population has become financially poorer and people's quality of life has diminished. When community centres are closed, when youth workers are sacked, when Sure Start centres close, when libraries are never open and school playing fields sold off, we are all much poorer. As always, it's the poor, the frail, the disabled and marginalised who, as well as being blamed for a poorly functioning economy, suffer the most from austerity, and the poverty they are forced into leads to exclusion.

When people are sanctioned by the Department for Work and Pensions, meaning their benefits are stopped, how do the makers of 'austerity politics' think they are to eat? But, of course, they're not seen as people, because those in government are usually so protected from poverty and the shame, fear, anxiety and suffering that goes with it, that the effects of their decisions are rarely realised. When a south-west MP was asked what he thought about the existence of food banks in his constituency he described them as 'uplifting'. I find this kind of disconnect and separation from people's suffering deeply disturbing, but part of a wider pattern of alienation.

DISCONNECTION

This kind of protected disconnection is, perhaps, seen most clearly in our society's refusal to take global warming and the disastrous legacy and future threats of climate change seriously. Like poverty for the rich and privileged, the catastrophic effects of climate change are not felt immediately in the UK. Few in our country are now foolish enough to deny or seek to contradict the conclusive scientific proof of climate change, yet as a nation we are in huge denial about the need to radically change our addictive consumption of fossil fuels and imagine and embrace cleaner and more sustainable ways of living.

When I was in the Solomon Islands in the South Pacific, living at a Franciscan friary, I used to join in with the brothers, who every Friday morning would 'do penance' for a couple of hours. This might involve litter picking in the environs of the friary and the surrounding villages; usually, though, it seemed to be clearing brush with a bush knife. Under the shadow of swaying coconut palms, to the sound of the ocean hitting the coral reef, everyone would form a line and clear whichever field, coconut grove or roadside verge needed it, and we'd resolutely hack away. I used to hate it, as within seconds I'd be dripping with sweat and the local ants, disturbed from their homes, would bite back. I complained about the ant bites to one of the brothers who told me not to worry: 'It only hurts for an hour and then the pain's gone.'

I didn't much like the idea of doing penance. It's a word seldom used in our affluent culture, where comfort, material security and wellbeing are so valued. Penance smacks of medievalism, hair shirts, flagellation and masochism to most of us in the West. I've often thought of its extreme forms as manifesting self-hatred or seeking to placate a fearsome punishing God who demands sacrifice. Yet when I joined in with the brothers 'doing penance', I was rather taken with this corporate act, a sense of saying sorry, a ritual everyday action to recognise our complicity in the things that go wrong in the world and in our distorted relationship with this earth, our common home. Hacking away, out in the open, suffering a little from the heat and insect bites, somehow connected me to the earth and systems of life we are hacking to pieces. Then I thought some more, and as I walked sweating towards the welcome cooling of the river, I suddenly realised that these brothers are amongst the last people in our world who should be doing penance, and trying, through their actions, to put things right in the world; rather, it should be people like me.

The average Solomon Islander has an almost imperceptible carbon footprint. Nearly everybody lives in a house constructed from wood, bamboo and sago palm for the roof. The only furniture in the house is likely to be sleeping mats woven out of coconut palm. The only possessions people have will be a change of clothes and some cooking pans, to use balanced on three stones over a wood fire. The diet is simple and gathered locally: fish, cassava, sweet potato, coconut, and maybe pork if there is a feast. The only things bought in would be rice and noodles. So simple, yet they're doing penance. The terrible irony is that it's the people of these islands and low-lying countries around the world who are the most badly affected by rises in sea level caused by the planet warming. Whilst I was there, a major hurricane wiped out half the houses on the island of Vanuatu, part of our road was washed away and a wing of the hospital in the capital, Honiara, disappeared into the sea.

Two weeks after I returned from the Solomons, I went on a huge parliamentary lobby in London organised by a number of major non-governmental organisations (NGOs) working in the aid and development fields, wishing to draw the attention of members of parliament to the devastating effects of global warming. There were so many people on the lobby that MPs had to see their constituents out in the street. A long line of thousands of constituents stretched through Parliament Gardens and all the way along the river and over Lambeth Bridge.

I'd travelled up with a coachful from West Dorset to lobby our MP, Sir Oliver Letwin. He rightly has a reputation as a fine constituency MP, getting things done locally and responding quickly and efficiently to requests for help from local people. He also has a formidable intellect, being described by a fellow Tory MP as having 'a brain the size of Venus', so he's a difficult man to lobby and win an argument with. The first time we lobbied him in the House of Commons, we left feeling stupid and somewhat patronised, so the next time we met him to argue for an increase in the international aid budget, I decided not to get into a clever argument but go for a passionate presentation of people's suffering in the developing world. This caught him off guard and rattled him and it felt like his defences had been lowered. Of course, there's a place for reasoned argument and careful consideration of the facts, but keeping everything cerebral can allow us to distance ourselves and cut ourselves off from the daily suffering people living in poverty have to endure. This lack of emotional connection can allow us to deny and separate ourselves from the consequences of the political choices we make.

We were waiting to meet him, as arranged, by Lambeth Bridge at 2 p.m. but there was no sign of him. So we rang his office and he agreed to come and see us for five minutes. Our group were furious at this apparent brush-off, after we'd travelled over 120 miles to meet him. We had a series of questions to ask him, but this was clearly going to be impossible, so I offered to give a short, dramatic, heartfelt speech outlining my very recent experiences of the effects of global warming in the Solomon Islands. He turned up and began to take control and organise us, promising two meetings back in West Dorset, letting us know how busy he was. As he was about to go, we surrounded him and asked for just five more minutes of his time. I began with what I thought was a passionate but respectful tirade at him about sea-level rising and cyclones in the Pacific, and our government's complacency over taking action to check global warming. The following day, Brother Hugh, who had been with me, produced a photo he'd taken with me leaning angrily towards Sir Oliver with my pointing finger just inches away from his nose.

I was shocked by this image, but not ashamed of my anger; far more alarming is the consistent complacency of governments and the lack of imagination and political will to address the single most pressing issue affecting our planet. It can only be by objectifying the earth and its myriad systems of life, and people like the Solomon Islanders, that we manage to deny the chaos already killing thousands, forcing the migration of millions of people and wiping out species and whole ecosystems. And this is only a tiny fraction of the suffering that is to come unless we can shake off our complacency. People like Oliver Letwin, like you and me, are not in denial about climate change, but I sometimes wonder whether we are in denial about the need to radically alter how we are to live if we are to reverse or at least slow down the rate the planet is warming, forests are being destroyed and the oceans are being polluted.

In his book *Climate: A New Story* (2018), Charles Eisenstein repeatedly stresses what he calls 'the story of separation' being the dominant narrative in the Western world, and what a disaster that has been for the earth. He argues that we need to develop a new way of thinking that sees the planet not as an inanimate object for us to use and abuse as we wish, but as a complex living system which we need to be in relationship with. He writes that until we understand this, no amount of reduction in the burning of fossil fuels will make any difference whilst we're still cutting down forests, ploughing up grasslands, draining wetlands, polluting the oceans and attacking the planet in numerous other ways:

Part of the mythology of separation is a belief in nature-as-thing: in other words, the belief that only human beings are possessed fully of self-hood. This is what licenses us to exploit the beings of nature, for our own ends, much as dehumanisation of brown people licensed light-skinned people to enslave them. (Eisenstein 2018, p.21)

If we seek to tackle global warming as the only environmental problem, then we give in to a way of thinking that Eisenstein calls separation and 'single issue' thinking. What's needed is a less disconnected approach that sees the earth as something alive and full of complex relationships of which we are part. He argues that until we begin seeing the earth as a living thing we belong to and which we are in relationship with, as indigenous people have always done, no amount of carbon sequestration or technical fixes will alter our headlong course to destruction.

Hope is to be found in challenging everything that leads us to alienation, by rediscovering a more relational way of connecting with one another and our planet. The tool that could help us most in this is relearning the art of accompaniment: a way of being with people and also with nature that fosters joy and interdependence, so challenging prevailing narratives of dominance and the need for individual autonomy at any cost. In some ways, adopting the practice of accompaniment can be seen as new and countercultural, but really it's a process of rediscovering a way of being that is embedded in indigenous cultures and in less 'developed' parts of the world. My encounter with the highly relational and communitarian culture of the Solomon Islands, and their deep sense of being part of the land and sea they inhabited, illustrated for me the joy and sustainability inherent in just learning to be with one another.

By choosing to live in two residential communities in the UK for the past 25 years, I've attempted to explore and live out a way of being with other people that diminishes the exclusion and objectification of people, and our disconnection from each other and the life around us. To learn to survive and then thrive in community, the thing that helped me most was learning to be comfortable just being with people, which is what I would describe as accompaniment.

When I arrived at Pilsdon Community, I spent the first year worrying that I should be doing more to help people change their lives and be rehabilitated. There was so much raw pain on display and bottled-up anger there that I also feared I would be crushed by the burden of it. How was I to survive without quickly burning out? How could I possibly be of use to so many people, often with multiple and complex needs?

Slowly, as I absorbed the culture of the place, I began to realise that the life there wasn't about 'making people better', but rather accepting them for who they were, with all their fallibilities and gifts. So many of our guests carried so much grief that it would have been impossible to fix their lives without a huge amount of therapeutic intervention, and yet, mysteriously, through the love, acceptance and order of community life, many people, as I did, began to thrive in community. I began to understand that no amount of endless listening from me, or me willing people to overcome their difficulties, would make much difference; it would only exhaust me. I began to see my role at Pilsdon as first being alongside individuals, not as a social worker, support worker or carer but simply as another human being, who gives and receives support simply by being there and sharing a common life. As Tobias Jones (2007, p.187), in his book *Utopian Dreams*, wrote after an extended visit to Pilsdon, 'We felt amazingly happy there because it's never pious or impious, it's just a bunch of people surviving together.'

Second, I saw my role there as one of the leadership team as creating and maintaining healthy community structures, which held people and allowed them to feel safe and, because of that, begin to let go of some of their fears. I also began to feel that my role was to accompany and be accompanied by not just individuals but the whole community: men, women, children, the animals and the land.

Living in community taught me that accompaniment is a reciprocal relationship. I learnt that to give people your time and learn to be with others in a way that seeks to be devoid of control or seeking to shape them, as well as building trust and a sense of belonging, is life-giving rather than draining. That's the wonder and the gift of accompaniment that living in community began to teach me. I began to learn that giving people time in a way that didn't force things or seek immediate outcomes or try to fix things, but rather concentrated on simply being present and enjoying being with the person, rather than being exhausting, energised me.

2

BEING IN COMMUNITY

I'm feeling anxious, sitting in a large 1960s assembly hall in a circle of about 60 people, over half of whom are long-term prisoners at Grendon prison, the only therapeutic prison in the country. We've had to go through the usual checks and searches to come in, but I'm struck by the very different atmosphere here to the other prisons I regularly go to in order to visit Gypsy and Traveller prisoners. In the other prisons, the first thing you feel is the stress which seems to bounce off the walls and is written into the faces of prisoners and staff alike. Last time I visited Guys Marsh prison, I only just managed to get in, as the prison was pretty much locked down because 16 prisoners had barricaded themselves into their wing, protesting the breakdown of the central heating, and the riot squad had been summoned. I got to the chapel, where I was due to meet my prisoners, by being escorted through a back entrance and past another wing which had been set on fire by the prisoners a few months earlier. The whole block was encased in corrugated iron sheeting and barbed wire, and seemed to symbolise the breakdown and the dereliction of relationships that led to people ending up in prison in the first place and the decay in a brutally underfunded system. An experienced chaplain told me that prisoners are constantly moved around prisons to stop them forming cliques, but this, in fact, breaks down any chance of building community between prisoners and staff. Staff too rarely stay long in the prison service; the average service of a newly qualified prison officer is down to 12 months. The advent of synthetic drugs such as 'spice' which are difficult to test for has led to prisoners' moods being highly unpredictable. What the chaplain said the prison service desperately needed was experienced staff and people willing to build a safe community for prisoners to live in, rather than the whole place lurching from one crisis to another.

Here at Grendon, we still do all the queuing up and going through multiple locked doors, but the atmosphere is much lighter. Many of the prisoners and staff smile at us and ask us how we are with genuine interest. I'm still feeling nervous though, as I'm about to give a presentation to a group of prisoners, prison chaplains, governors and other prison staff from around the country on the theme, 'Concepts of Community'. My stress level has been ratcheted up after Father Christopher Jamison, monk, TV star and former abbot of Worth Abbey, a Benedictine community featured in the Channel 4 series *The Monastery*, has given a brilliant and witty paper on the similarities between monastic life and being in prison. Worse still for me, this was followed by a moving and brutally honest testimony by a prisoner named James, who began by saying, 'I killed an elderly man when I was 17,' and went on not to justify his crime, for which he was full of remorse, but to tell his story up to and after the murder and outline the therapeutic process he'd been through for the past five years, a large part of which was living intentionally in community with the other prisoners on the wing. I'd rarely heard anyone speak with such raw emotional honesty or such profound insight.

'My God, how do I follow that?' I'm thinking, and then, as I walk to the podium, it comes to me: 'Just follow the script and trust in your experience for the last 20-odd years, and look at the prisoners, and speak to them, not the highly trained experts.' So I do this, and quickly the 20 minutes have passed and people are now really engaging me with questions.

At Grendon I talked about six fundamental building blocks of community, which have sustained me and the communities I've lived in over the years, which are: vision, boundaries, generosity, trust, need and celebration. They each contain aspects of accompaniment, as each aspect contains within it the intention to seek to be with others, and build interdependence, which is at the heart of the process of accompaniment. The pursuit of independence is probably what has led to the growth of loneliness and exclusion, and what community life, at its best, offers is the security of belonging to and being part of something much bigger than ourselves. The building of strong and sustainable community is the antidote to loneliness and marginalisation, and is made up of these six characteristics.

VISION

In the Jewish scriptures, the Book of Proverbs says that 'the people without a vision will perish'. What binds a community together is a shared sense of belonging, which comes from being able to articulate and live out a common vision. It's something to go back to when conflicts inevitably arise, or tiredness and disillusionment set in. If people have captured the vision of the community and share the values arising from it, then much can be overcome and if the vision is powerful enough, it will constantly renew and re-enchant old and new community members.

In her book *Pilsdon Morning*, Gaynor Smith, joint founder of the Pilsdon Community with her husband Percy, tells of how many people came to Pilsdon saying, 'we're thinking of founding a community, what do you advise?' (1982, p.27). Her advice was not to spend too long thinking about it, but just to plunge into it trusting in your initial vision. I've had many people say to me how they and a couple of friends want to start a community. I will quickly try and tell them, it's not friendship that builds a community but a common vision; sadly, many apparently strong friendships have foundered under the strains of living together. 'What's your inspiration for living in community and what will be your shared values?' I always ask.

At Pilsdon, I was always strongly aware of Percy Smith's vision for the community, based on the three principles of prayer, simple manual work and the welcome of others, continuing to guide us. When things got tough or people challenged our community life,

I learnt to find a way forward by measuring each challenge against these core principles and activities of the community. Unlike a monastic community, we had no written rule, only an oral tradition, but such was the strength of Percy's original vision that 60 years later the community continues in much the same manner as in its early years.

Percy's vision of Pilsdon had been inspired by the life of the seventeenth-century Little Gidding community founded by Nicholas Ferrar. Nicholas Ferrar, fellow of Clare College, Cambridge, had been a major shareholder of the Virginia Company, and on a visit to the New World had begun planning for a new university in the Americas which would include British, French and Spanish settlers and Native Americans – an idea sadly so far ahead of his time that it was never instituted. He was an MP and tipped to have a glittering career in Parliament, but in 1625 he resigned his seat in order to establish a community based around the manor house in the hamlet of Little Gidding in Huntingdonshire. The community was based around his extended family: his mother, his brother, his brother's wife and children, and his sister, her husband and their children. Twice a day, the family would walk over to the little church and pray morning and evening prayer. They farmed the ten acres of land around the manor house and welcomed visitors 'both high and low'. The community was made famous in the twentieth century through the poem 'Little Gidding', one of T. S. Elliot's *Four Quartets*. There's a beautifully crafted black-and-white film of Pilsdon, made by the BBC in 1968, in which Percy says he stood at the tomb of Nicholas Ferrar in Little Gidding, where he 'became utterly convinced by the sanity of their way of life'. Today, at Pilsdon, those two visions continue to permeate the place as does the smell of Golden Virginia tobacco from the Americas, fittingly the most popular brand smoked in copious quantities by today's Pilsdon guests.

The vision of Pilsdon has inspired a sister community in the enclosure of a Benedictine community of sisters at West Malling in Kent, and Windsor Hill Wood, a community based in Shepton Mallet, living a life of prayer, woodland work and the welcome of visitors. All my time at Pilsdon, I felt that the vision of the place accompanied me; it was something so strong you could almost feel it.

Vision, too, can be lost or too difficult to sustain, as seemed to happen some years ago at Hilfield Friary, where I now live. Hilfield had been created out of the vision of Brother Giles in 1921, as a place where men of the road could find a place to settle and learn to belong again. Back in 1921, there was a huge need for such a place of recovery with over 60,000 thousand men on the road, many suffering from 'shell shock', or what we would now call post-traumatic stress disorder, as a result of fighting in the First World War, and many others made homeless by the post-war economic collapse. Brother Giles soon left, following a scandal when he was caught kissing another man, and the inspiration for the work with the hundreds of men who came every year came from Brother Douglas. Brother Douglas worked alongside the wayfarers in the large vegetable garden, growing food and seeking to grow hospitality and friendship and restore people's confidence. He had a vision for a 'Home of St Francis' in every county and a house of hospitality in every major city, and managed to found at least eight such places. He campaigned effectively for the repeal of the punitive 1834 Poor Laws, and every time he went up to London to lobby Parliament, he would sleep overnight with other rough sleepers in the crypt of St Martin's in the Fields in Trafalgar Square. His vision had been inspired by his admiration for St Francis of Assisi (1182–1226), who in turn was inspired by the itinerant ministry of Jesus amongst the poor and marginalised.

For over 70 years, Hilfield Friary had opened its doors to wayfarers, but by 2005, due to a lack of brothers, the community reluctantly closed its night-shelter and hospitality to the homeless. With the loss of the ministry to wayfarers, the friary seemed to lose its vital vision and began to founder. Guests still came, but the depleted and ageing group of brothers were struggling to cope with them, as they were with Brother Douglas' beloved vegetable garden and the 20 acres of land, which were becoming overgrown. The place either had to be closed or reimagined.

Fortunately, Brother Sam became guardian, with a new vision for Hilfield as a mixed community of brothers and lay people, who lived with an emphasis on living simply and sustainably, and on environmental justice, work on the land, work with people of other faiths, and re-establishing work with the socially excluded. Ten years on, the community is thriving again, with six Franciscan brothers, three married couples, four children, and six volunteers from around the world in their early twenties sharing community life with a rich variety of visitors. The bells still ring, and several brown-habited friars shuffle into chapel four times a day joined by a mix of others. The vegetable garden yields abundantly, and in early summer, wildflower meadows are abloom with eight species of orchids; sheep, cattle and pigs all graze the land, new trees are being planted for the biomass boiler which heats the houses, and a vibrant community meets around a common table three times a day.

A vision had been lost, but a new vision has been established and articulated – an expanded and more interconnected vision, still faithful to the way of St Francis.

BOUNDARIES

Central to life at the Friary are the bells that mark out and boundary the day. Someone rings the wake-up bell at 6.45 a.m., then another rings for morning prayer at 7.30 a.m., then another for breakfast at 8 a.m., and so on throughout the day, the last being for night prayer at 9 p.m. The ringing of bells in a way compartmentalises time and gives a discipline, but most of all a rhythm, to friary life. Without boundaries, it would be hard to sustain the life and vision of a community for long.

In my talk at Grendon prison, the part I noticed the prisoners most engaged with was when I began to speak about boundaries. Good parenting provides clear boundaries, which allow the child to feel safe and know that someone cares about them by giving consistent messages about how to relate well and positively to others and the world around them. As some of the prisoners told their stories, it became clear that, for most of them from their early years, they had never had clear boundaries. The prison system, of course, like the monastery described by Father Chris Jamison, has a highly delineated structure. Lines not to be crossed are drawn on the floor, steel bars separate areas, meals are served at the same time each day, and often the same food on the same days of the week; work times, exercise times, recreation times are all clearly boundaried. I've met a number of long-term prisoners who on release have really struggled to cope with the loss of routine and lack of discipline in the outside world, and I've even known some who have committed further crimes in order to return to the 'safety' of the prison system.

We all need to know where we are, and at a deep level to feel held, and for many in our society there's an absence of that inner sense of security or the sense of belonging to a community. With the minimal nurture and setting of boundaries in early years, and the erosion of communities and institutions to build community, it's no wonder that we live in an age where so many people struggle to feel they belong or feel safe anywhere.

Many who came to Pilsdon began to grow and develop, supported by the rules of community life. There was a lovely man called Rob who had had a chaotic life. As a child he'd been in care, followed by borstal, then prison, and when out of prison he drank heavily, whilst living on the streets. He came to us through his Alcoholics Anonymous sponsor, who was running a group with prisoners. I went to visit him inside, and met a big man whose broken nose and scarred face and LOVE and HATE tattooed on the knuckles of either hand spoke of the battles of his past, but when I began describing Pilsdon and talked of our pigs, I saw a look of such tenderness fill his face that I knew we should take a risk and invite him to the community. He came and looked after the pigs with great devotion, and became a regular early-morning milker of our Jersey cows. His love for the pigs bordered on the obsessive and he would recount in great detail what our sows Ivy or Cacophonia had been up to each day. He was also brilliant at sitting with and supporting newly arrived guests who were feeling a bit shaky and perhaps also physically trembling as they came off the drink. For Rob it was the rules that kept him safe, because he knew that we'd ask him to leave immediately if he drank, and the threat of this kept him abstinent. The pattern of each day, shaped around the milking, feeding and mucking out of animals, also gave him an extra sense of security. He knew he also had to keep his temper in check because we had zero tolerance of violence and threats of violence in the community, and occasionally he sailed pretty close to the wind. I remember on one occasion, after he had a row with one of the other guests, I followed him into one of the barns where he'd gone to calm down. He turned to look at me with tears in his eyes. 'I'm a bastard, you know,' he said.

'No you're not!' I replied

'I'm a bastard, a bastard,' he insisted.

'No you're not,' I re-emphasised. 'You may be difficult at times, but I'd never describe you as a bastard.'

'No, I'm a *bastard*, legitimate or something.'

'Aah...I understand,' I replied. 'You don't need to worry about that, lots of people are born illegitimate these days. You're just big Rob to us, the best pig man Pilsdon has ever had.'

When people came to stay at Pilsdon I would go through with them what I called the 'Magnificent Seven' boundaries which were not to be transgressed.

1. Come to all meals, as that's the one time the whole community gets together.
2. Join in the work of the place, as you are able.
3. It's a 'dry' house, so anyone under the influence of drink or non-prescribed drugs will be asked to leave immediately.
4. No violence or intimidation.
5. No exclusive relationships to be formed, as our experience shows these seldom work out and are disruptive of community life.
6. If you are on prescribed medication you need to keep taking it, unless the doctor agrees to changes.
7. For the first three months you don't go away overnight.

This perhaps sounds very institutional, but I think that having these core boundaries allowed people to feel secure in the knowledge that we had expectations of them and that behaviour that threatened the life of the community would not be tolerated. Boundaries, of course, are all very well, but for them to mean anything they have to be enforced and that was the role of the leader and community members. The first weekend I arrived, I asked three people to leave, two for drinking and the third for smoking heroin. It was as though I was being tested, and once people knew I could be tough, everyone felt safe again. It was as though a new parental figure had come in and could be trusted to hold the boundaries.

It was usually people under the influence of alcohol or drugs who were asked to leave, and I felt no sense of guilt about putting somebody out who had transgressed the rule, as I knew I had clearly laid down the boundaries with them, and that, in excluding them, I was helping keep the rest of the community safe. Of course, we would try and help people find a new place to go to and would sometimes readmit them to the community if we thought they had a chance of keeping sober for the next few months. Sometimes people I'd thrown out would return and thank me for doing so, as it had brought them to their senses and they'd gone on to seek extra support for their addiction. How did we know someone had been drinking or using drugs? Simple, we had a breathalyser kit and a urine test, and once these were produced the person in denial would invariably admit to their inebriation without a test. Holding the boundaries around drink, drugs and violence helped people be safe and, in turn, more at home with each other. In my accompaniment of others, I'm also aware of the need to keep certain boundaries in my walking alongside them. They may be about confidentiality, around not slipping into the temptation to try and fix things for people, promising too much or not setting limits on the time I give to people. For people to feel safe with me, I also need to feel safe with them.

Pilsdon also felt safe because of its physical containment. It was seven miles from the nearest town, its northern side was flanked by hills, the farmyard enclosed by buildings, and the south-facing front of the house bounded by a garden wall. It was a place of asylum in the best sense and it reminded me of the old county asylums the Victorians had built. I visited the county asylum in Lincoln in 1986 just as it was being sold off to developers and the final wards shut. It was a vast and somewhat forbidding place, with one corridor nearly a quarter of a mile long, and there were some residents who'd become totally institutionalised by it; it was right that it needed to be replaced by more integrated care in the community. Sadly, the whole government policy of community care seemed to be driven as much by the need to save money as by a vision of a more humane system. As I got to know former patients of the asylum in a day centre for those now living in the community, I noticed that nearly all of them were nostalgic for the old hospital. The hospital had had a large vegetable garden, a laundry and a chapel, and built its own coffins; patients could walk endlessly round the ten acres of grounds in the open countryside, feeling safe and contained behind its walls. Now I heard descriptions of people staying in bed all day in their solitary flats just staring at the bedroom wall, afraid to go out and desperately lonely. At the day centre, people would speak with affection of the eccentric behaviour of patients on the ward and the idiosyncrasies of the staff. The day centre they now attended was a lifeline, but only there two days a week, and a number of people didn't always feel well enough to go there. I remember one 60-year-old man telling me about basket making in the old asylum, joking that it was for 'basket cases', but expressing how much he enjoyed the discipline of sitting down with others and making something. The image of the basket has stayed with me and I think that strong communities need to be like a woven basket, weaving people together, and places of containment in the sense that people can choose to be and feel safe in the knowledge of shared values, which respect the needs of the individual and the needs of the whole community.

In our fragmented world there's a greater need than ever to create places of belonging where people can feel held and safe. The drive towards efficiency in public services, and the emphasis on individual choice, has led in some instances to a breakdown of community. I was amazed when we were being inspected at Pilsdon under the government programme Supporting People, which partly funded the community, when the inspectors turned down our invitation to lunch. I explained to them the importance of meals in our community life, and that they wouldn't really understand the community without coming to lunch. However, they refused on the grounds that it might influence the impartiality of their decision making. The acceptance of a free lunch could be seen as us seeking to influence the inspectors and was a boundary they were not prepared to cross. A few weeks later, I got my own back on the inspectors when, at a plenary session of a Supporting People conference, I asked how they quantified the outcomes of the work our two donkeys, Peter and Paul, did with our residents. The panel looked at one another and finally decided the benefits of looking after donkeys provided 'soft outcomes'.

Boundaries can have a negative effect on community if they are applied too formally and institutionally. Writing in *The Guardian*, Nicci Gerrard (2017) tells how disastrous a short stay in hospital was for her father:

> When he went into hospital, he was living with dementia, happy and beloved and linked to his world by a thousand invisible threads. Restricted visiting and a lockdown of his ward because of norovirus meant that, one by one, those delicate threads were cut. When he came out five weeks later, he was no longer living with dementia but dying with it: a radically slowed-down death and a harrowing way to say goodbye.

Boundaries and professional standards are undoubtedly necessary in our world for institutions to function and people to flourish, but they definitely need to be tempered by my third mark of community, which I call generosity.

GENEROSITY

Pilsdon always tried to be generous in allowing people who had previously left and failed at independent living to return to the community; if we felt there was something they could contribute to the community and that they could grow and develop by being with us again, we would often say yes, because we didn't really believe in independent living. We saw how it would too often lead to loneliness and sometimes premature death.

One of our guests at Pilsdon was called Tony, and the day we picked him up from the railway station he looked as though he was close to death. It took two of us to hoist him into the back of the minibus, so fragile was his state. After a couple of days, he said he was ready to do a bit of work and we suggested he help with laying tables in the dining room. Soon he'd become a kind of maître d' and he loved running the dining room like a military operation. It transpired he'd been an officer in the army intelligence section; a rumour soon began to circulate that he'd been a spy, and he became known as the 'Wing Commander'. He had a well-lived-in face for his 50-odd years, heavy jowls and bulging eyes, which sparkled when he saw the funny side of something or someone lovingly ribbed him. He smoked over 40 cigarettes a day, and each time he laughed it always seemed to end in a fit of choking. It was drink that had led to his downfall. He'd been married three times and had owned four restaurants, which had all lost money. Given the support of the community, he stayed sober and thrived in his role of generous welcomer to guests to the dining room, where he built up a team of at least three people working for him – someone to lay the tables, someone to help clear up and even a flower arranger for each table. In his fourth year with us he decided to leave and set himself up in a flat.

We moved him into the new place, and then three months later we were carrying the furniture out again, as in a matter of months he'd drunk himself to death. As we carried out a particularly heavy mahogany wardrobe, it felt like we were carrying out his coffin. At his funeral, his estranged daughter said she didn't recognise the fine man described throughout the Pilsdon service, which, as always, was full of generous praise and brutal honesty about the deceased. I remember saying to her that living in community could bring out the best in people if people were able to commit generously to the life, as Tony had, and give of their time to being with others.

When talking about community at Hilfield Friary, the guardian, Brother Sam, would emphasise the need for 'bucket loads and bucket loads of generosity'. It's not easy living in close proximity to people who are inevitably different to you, but may also remind you of all the things you don't like about yourself. At Hilfield, we have to meet each other three times a day over the dining table, work together, walk past each other several times a day, and share common space. Sometimes it seems there's no respite from one another, and without 'bucket loads of generosity' and learning to love the fallibilities of others and our own weaknesses, community life would be a nightmare. It seems that the longer people have been in the community, generally the better they are at life together. It must be something about generosity compounding itself. Brother Hugh, who's lived in community for nearly 40 years, models a willing kind of generosity for the whole community. He's always the first to volunteer for house cleaning, working with the more difficult cook in the kitchen, or picking someone up from the station. He's always there at the end of the day in the kitchen to help with the final task of mopping the floor. Two of his favourite jobs are the vilest smelling – cleaning the fat trap, and looking after the sewage system – and he's always enthusiastically offering to let others help him, but seldom is his offer taken up.

Brother Hugh is equally generous in his assessment of others, very slow to say anything negative, and always looking to find the funny side of any situation. We both share a high regard for the 'Bruderhof', an Anabaptist community with large settlements in Kent and Sussex. The community was founded by Eberhard Arnold in Germany during the late 1920s. It was persecuted by the Nazis and forced to flee to the UK and USA. They now have over 4000 members, about 700 of whom live in Kent and Sussex. They take the teachings of the New Testament strongly to heart, so are active pacifists and live from a common purse without private possessions, so when individuals join, they give away any private wealth and individual autonomy in obedience to the common will of the community. When I have visited, I've been hugely impressed by their kindness and generosity to one another. 'Need a hand with that?' is the most common phrase used, but they have one rule that is sacrosanct and vital to the building up of community life. They call it the 'law of love', which stipulates you should never talk about anyone behind their back; you should always seek to address people directly and if you have a problem with one of the community, you shouldn't complain to another about them but speak frankly to that person; this leads to a growth in trust, the deepening of relationships and an honesty with one another, and of course cuts out gossip, which is so destructive to all human relationships. It's something I aspire to, and I'm learning through the good example of those who've lived in community a long time to keep my counsel when someone upsets me rather than immediately responding defensively or angrily or complaining behind their back. This can buy time and allow me to process things and work out what it is that has upset me in the encounter and establish what belongs to them and what I might be projecting onto them. Then it might be important to go back and, with generosity and openness, challenge the person about their words or behaviour. In the therapeutic communities that make up the wings of Grendon prison there was the same insistence on the need for each prisoner to talk openly and honestly about his feelings and to be prepared to be vulnerable with one another, which could only work if the whole community generously bought into a culture of rigorous honesty.

The Bruderhof support their UK communities by producing high-quality play equipment, and everyone from the age of 12 works in their factory for at least part of the day. I'd never been anywhere where individual will was sacrificed for the common good or seen such communality until I went to the Solomon Islands in the Pacific. Like the Bruderhof, Solomon Islands culture is strongly communitarian, and people there have a natural capacity to share. The first day I worked outdoors in a clearing, planting cassava, I was amazed to see how everything was organised. Under swaying coconut palms with the sound of the Pacific breaking on the reef, sweat pouring down my back, I noticed how no one was in charge, nobody gave out any orders. People just got on with the job, clearing any vegetation with bush knives, hoeing up mounds in which to plant the sticks of cassava, and cutting lengths to be planted, with someone pushing them into the soil and, of course, someone to climb a coconut tree to provide refreshment. It seemed that everyone worked as one. If someone got tired, they rested, and no one gave them a hard time or barbed banter. No boss, nobody marking out lines or boundaries, just everyone joining in and working as one.

A couple of weeks later, part of the road linking the Franciscan friary to Honiara, the capital, was washed away as the river flooded, and a bunch of primary school children were stuck on the wrong side of the flood and unable to get home. So the brothers threw a rope across the floodwaters and used it to guide themselves through chest-high water, and then raised each child onto their shoulders and guided them across. The next morning the flood had subsided, but part of the road had been washed away, so we spent the morning taking flat and rounded stones from the riverbed, and rebuilt it as best we could. Hard labour, but immensely satisfying, and again the 20 or so of us working as one.

The following day I was coming back from town in the community truck when as we arrived back at the bridge ready to cross our newly laid road, we were flagged down by a couple of red-eyed villagers with bush knives. 'You'll have to pay a charge to cross the road we repaired,' they demanded.

'No way!' I replied angrily, jumping out of the truck. 'You had nothing to do with rebuilding the road! It was the brothers, and I helped them!'

We drove over our new road, proudly but gingerly without payment. The brothers in the back of the truck laughed and laughed at my outrage, saying, 'All you had to do was tell them we were brothers from the friary and they would have let us through. The easygoing nature of the brothers and their generosity in rebuilding the road seemed to contrast with that of the toll collectors, who seemed to represent the values of individualistic capitalism that were slowly seeping into the islands, where most people still lived lives of mutual interdependence.

One of the things I really value in the community of Hilfield is that, although we live in Dorset, one of the least culturally diverse parts of Britain, the community always has a strong international flavour. People from India, China, South Korea, Papua New Guinea, South Africa, Nigeria, Uganda, the Czech Republic, Hungary, Slovenia, Italy, Germany, Belgium and North America all sit around our common table. Our oldest member is 86 and the youngest is three, and, of course, they all have a range of personalities and different backgrounds. Our diversity makes us strong: just as we know that the strongest ecosystems are the ones with the most biodiversity, so communities that can generously embrace difference tend to thrive. The political narratives that seek to divide communities, by 'othering' and scapegoating people by labelling them as 'welfare scroungers' or 'swarms of refugees', inevitably lead to a weaker, divided and fearful society.

For a community to grow, develop and include others, a deep sense of gratitude for what we have and where we belong is essential, and if we realise that all of life is a gift to be shared generously with others then community will inevitably grow. Vital to living generously is the practice of humility. So much of the story we're told in the West is that it's vital to build up self-reliance, material security in the form of property and possessions, and status, and that the role of government is to protect these. What community living continues to teach me is that this craving for physical and emotional security is bogus and always seems to divide people. Time and again the virtue that seems to break down difference and conflict in community is humility.

I can still hear Percy Smith, founder of Pilsdon, repeating one of his favourite sayings, 'Not one of us is better than another. We are all in equal need of God's mercy.' If we're generous with ourselves and are honest about our own fallibilities, then we can be more generous with the faults of others. A question I often ask myself when I'm angry or find profound feelings of dislike surfacing towards another person is, 'What part of me that I don't like is being triggered by this person?' It sometimes takes a bit of processing to work it out, but when I do, I'm grateful because I find my anger against the other transformed into compassion. Compassion both for them and for that part of myself I'm uncomfortable with. Sometimes this compassion takes a bit of time to arrive, other times it comes almost immediately.

There was a man in my early days at Pilsdon called Graham, who I took a profound dislike to, and all I thought I could do was keep away from him as much as possible and wait for him to leave. He had been in the army, and used to strut around, looking important, and constantly tell everyone about his expertise as a handyman. He was fairly loud, had a slightly put-on Belfast accent, was sexist, angry, prickly and would push people around who were weaker than him. He really got to me. After about a year of skirting round him, I'd finally had enough. He began picking on the cook, who'd been invalided out of the Navy suffering post-traumatic stress disorder after the Falklands War, and used to shake a lot. I intervened, ready to shout and vent my months of frustration. Graham stormed off before I could take him on and, still furious, I hurried after him, following him through the farmyard and cornering him in the community workshop. As I burst through the door, I was surprised to see his eyes full of tears. We sat down and he told me his story.

He'd grown up in Belfast, with family life dominated by a violent and alcoholic father, but at the age of 16 he'd got a job at Shorts, a local factory, making and servicing sewing machines, and he told me of his pride when he gave his first wage packet to his mother. Soon after, his father got work in England, and though he begged to stay, he was forced to move to another country, which was hugely anti-Irish following the IRA bombing campaign of the 1970s. He endured constant abuse as a young man, which continued in the army. He'd never got over what he described as being 'ripped away from' Belfast, and with a failed marriage, and discharge from the army, which had given him a strong sense of belonging, his drinking got worse and he ended up living on the street. 'I always kept my accent up,' he told me, 'even though I took a few beatings for it, as I'm proud of where I come from.'

As he spoke, tears also filled my eyes, and I finally began to understand him, what had shaped him and some of our common ground. Like him, I have a mother from Belfast; like him, I tend to repress my feelings, and an insecure part of me sometimes questions where I belong. I felt humbled by our conversation and strangely comforted that I now knew him better, and also part of myself, too. We never became great friends, but a new kind of respect had grown between us. Nowadays, going into difficult conversations with people, particularly those I struggle with, I try to listen and speak from a place of humility, a place of vulnerability, realising that, as with me, there's always more to a person than that which they present to the world. I'm constantly learning that humility is an essential ingredient of accompaniment, as by reducing the amount of space my ego and certainties take up in any encounter, more room is made for the other. In my encounter with Graham, the shock of his tears, which touched into my own vulnerabilities, allowed me to make the space for him to be able to talk. Generosity and humility allow us to better accompany others. Humility is more likely to build trust and encourage the honesty that makes relationships more real.

TRUST

Trust is another of the vital elements to building community. There's a Dutch saying that 'Trust arrives slowly on foot, but leaves rapidly on horseback.' Nationally and internationally there seems to have been an erosion of trust in public institutions and public figures. The banking crisis, Brexit and the election of Donald Trump all point to an alarming breakdown in trust in economic and governmental institutions. I would argue that a lot of this stems from the breakdown of local community and common bonds, through the growth of individualism and consumerism. The local bank manager used to live in the community and would know, or know of, the customer who came to ask for a loan. Nowadays, you apply online or see a business manager, who is seldom in the same job for more than a couple of years and is incentivised to sell loans and mortgages rather than serve the customer. Members of parliament often used to have worked in their local community, in business and industry, or in public services; now a majority come from jobs in law, the media and political parties. In 2011, someone remarked that the Archbishop of Canterbury, a former oil executive, knew more about business, industry and economics than the then Chancellor of the Exchequer. With cuts of over 40 per cent in government funding of local authorities since 2010, the breakdown of trust and participation in local government has been further eroded, and their ability to support and build trust with local community organisations has massively diminished. There are, of course, examples that buck the trend, such as the credit union movement, which promotes small local lending banks dependent on a 'common bond'. Local lunch clubs that support growing numbers of elderly and isolated people in rural and urban locations now abound, restoring trust and relationships to combat isolation. Living well in the places I've lived seems dependent on generous and trusting relationships. If you know you can rely on someone to do a job, or cope well with a difficult individual, it makes all the difference; conversely if people don't do what they say they will or clash or undermine another person, it can rapidly destabilise a community.

At Pilsdon, the worst thing you could do for a newly arrived person in recovery from addiction was to trust them too much. It was helpful for people in their first few weeks to know that the whole community was keeping an eye on them and that if they started drinking again or using drugs, people would know and they'd be excluded. The enforcement of this boundary paradoxically seemed to build trust, as people felt safe knowing there was zero tolerance of drinking and all the chaos and destructive behaviour it can bring. As people grew into their sobriety, so they learnt to trust others more and were ready to take on more responsibility in the community. Of course, we had regular breaches of trust where someone would have to be asked to leave or temporarily excluded, but this seemed to reinforce, for those who remained, that they were trusted as long as they kept within the discipline of community life.

At Pilsdon, each weekend brought several wayfarers for temporary stays at the community, and for some of the settled guests of the community, welcoming them in could be challenging. The wayfarers were often free spirits and some had multiple difficulties, so they would need firm and loving handling. One summer's evening, most of the fit and able members of the community were out playing for or watching the Pilsdon cricket team, when a very drunk and aggressive former resident turned up. He barged his way into the kitchen demanding food, which people gladly gave him before gently asking him to leave, as he was very obviously drunk. He refused, threatening violence. He was a big man, and potentially dangerous, so the two women minding the community called the police. Before the police arrived, he terrorised the few people left in the community, throwing furniture round one of the community rooms and smashing its windows. As soon as the police turned up, he suddenly calmed down and was back to his usual charming self and went away willingly.

His visit had left some of the more vulnerable members of the community shaken, and I heard mutterings about how we should stop taking in wayfarers, which concerned me. The next day, I'd gone into town to pick up replacement glass for the broken windows, when I picked up two new wayfarers walking to the community, one of whom had been a builder, before his drinking had lost him his job. I told them the story of our last wayfarer, which angered them, and almost as soon as they'd put their bags down, they set to work repairing the windows with great willingness. Throughout the day, people walked past our new repair crew, and it was as though the restoration of the windows by these two wayfarers was a restoration of trust in wayfarers as a whole.

Trusting someone to do a job was also a good way to build people's confidence and make them feel part of the community. To ask someone to look after the chickens meant you were trusting them with the animals' welfare. They'd have to get up in the morning to let the chickens out, check they had food, water and clean bedding, collect the eggs later in the day and remember to lock them away for the evening to keep the fox away. At Pilsdon we had a young man, Greg, who came to us with what he described as social phobia, and he would regularly self-harm by cutting himself. Greg was bright and articulate and knew that to progress in life he needed to face up to his self-imposed isolation, so he confronted it by joining our community. The first few weeks were difficult for him and he still cut himself, which we calmly accepted, just providing him with dressings and bandages for his wounds, not making a big drama of it, and not threatening to ask him to leave. This seemed to help him, and his self-harm began to decrease, but the thing that helped him most was when we asked him to look after our two scabby old donkeys. Greg had a tiny whisper of a voice and when I asked him if he could take on looking after the donkeys he muttered hesitantly, 'But will they like me?'

'But of course they will!' I boomed back at him. 'As long as you give them food and water, do their feet, brush their backs, stroke their necks and give them an occasional ginger nut biscuit, they won't just like you, they'll love you!'

From the moment he started looking after the donkeys, Greg seemed to thrive on the new responsibility and trust conferred on him. Six months later he'd left the community full of confidence, intending to train as a nurse and begin binding up the wounds of others.

At Grendon prison James, the prisoner mentioned earlier in this chapter, said to me that one of the most difficult parts of the whole therapeutic process was learning to trust others with your innermost fears; so many of the prisoners, like him, had been so badly let down by parents and adults throughout their childhoods, leaving them deeply wounded and struggling to trust. He said, 'Once I began sharing in a group and heard others tell me of their own experiences of abandonment, I suddenly realised I wasn't the only one. It was a revelation. I thought, till then, there was something wrong with me, it was my fault, but I began to realise I wasn't alone and that's when my life began to change. For the first time I could share my story with others who I knew would understand me.'

When I became leader of Pilsdon, I knew that building trust between me and my core team of five or six community members was a vital part of my role, and without mutual trust we would struggle. We already had a group supervision session once a month with an outside consultant, which allowed us to share difficulties faced in the community as a whole and in the dynamics of our core group. To this, I added one-to-one supervision, which I did monthly with each community member. These two kinds of support were vital in allowing a safe place where people could be very honest about their struggles and needs in a safe and confidential atmosphere. Making the time to listen to people on a regular basis is a vital way of affirming and building up individuals who, in turn, will build up community. Good accompaniment builds trust, and the building of trust strengthens community.

NEED

People never join communities out of pure altruism but because of their own needs, and knowing your own need and being able to support the needs of others is a vital part of building up community. My experience is that communities work best when people are able to be honest about their own needs and reasons for being in community and their need of others. Today, so many of the places that should be natural communities arising out of the need for mutuality, such as our schools, health services, public utilities and even charities, now run on a model that places achievement, financial efficiency, value for money and competitiveness as their primary driving forces. Of course, competence is vital for any agency supporting those in need, but it's compassion and a sense of togetherness that build resilient communities.

An example of this would be the probation service, which over the past 25 years has dramatically changed for the worse. Probation officers, 25 years ago, would regularly go out and visit their clients and initiate projects in the community, had budgets to support individuals and would work with a variety of agents in the community. Nowadays, probation officers are largely deskbound, writing court reports and risk assessments, and have no discretionary budgets. Any community projects they used to run with ex-offenders have been awarded to private companies, with an emphasis on financial profit. The role of the probation officer has moved from the care and rehabilitation of offenders to an emphasis on public protection. There's now little room for discretion or tailoring services towards the needs of individuals or communities, but rather public services are based on meeting their legal requirements and hitting their targets.

Communities aren't built up by ticking all the right boxes but by real engagement with each other and knowing each other's needs. Really good community work comes out of listening to the needs of a community and encouraging that community to articulate its needs and come up with its own solutions.

At Pilsdon, there was a very high degree of acceptance of people, in spite of their faults, as so many who found their way there had suffered great loss and been wounded by life. The one kind of person no one there could stand, and would have no time for, was the man or woman who would not admit to their need for support: the person who would blame others for their predicament, who was in denial about their drinking, or would refuse to show any weakness. But if they could get over their pride and honestly admit how messed up their life had become, there was a huge amount of empathy and mutual solidarity which would come their way. Knowing our need of one another is foundational for any kind of community building. When we manage to share our vulnerabilities with one another, it always seems more authentic than sharing our successes and achievements. Success and achievement too often separate us from one another, whilst our failures are much more likely to bind us together.

Communities seem to work best when there is a real need for extra pairs of hands to make them work. One of the reasons so many guests keep returning to Hilfield Friary is that it's not set up as a guest house or a retreat centre, but a community. Visitors are encouraged to join in our life. The community cooks for our guests, but visitors can help with picking veg from the garden and preparing it, then join in the washing-up afterwards. Others might join in with hedge laying, weeding, a bit of decorating, sweeping the yard, making some beds, doing some sewing or helping to stuff some envelopes. Everyone is invited to our morning meeting, when the day's work is planned and volunteers can be taken on. Most people only stay a few days, but the experience of working alongside others and performing some much-needed tasks gives them a real sense of belonging to the community.

A story is told of the Abbe Pierre, a French priest, social activist and campaigner for the homeless, who, when confronted by a man who was threatening to take his own life, asked him to hang on for a moment as he needed his help. At Pilsdon, the place utterly depended on the involvement of the guests to keep the place running. Any jobs people took on were real jobs, and there were always gaps to be filled. We often began building projects in faith, just hoping the person with the right skills would come along, and almost always they did. I'd just put in the foundations for a new bungalow when Mike turned up, who told me he was a plasterer. 'That'll be good as we get near the end,' I said, 'but I was really hoping you were a bricklayer.'

'Oh, I can do that too,' he replied, and three days later the walls were up and we began on the roof timbers. Mike stayed with us till the building was complete and it was a lovely job for him, as he hadn't worked for several years and he grew in confidence as the building went up around him. Occasionally, the right person didn't come along or was asked to leave midway through a job, but this was also an opportunity to ask friends or a local builder whether they could offer help or advice, and it always seemed to strengthen and develop relationships.

We began talking about 'sustainable vulnerability' at Pilsdon, as a foundational theme of our life. I came to understand that if the community became too organised and competent and we paid people to do jobs for us, or didn't rely on our guests enough for core tasks, the community would be in danger of becoming institutionalised and begin excluding people. If, however, we took on too many people with very complex needs and tried to do too many different projects, the community would become unstable and exhausting for people. It was really important that Pilsdon remained slightly fragile as an organisation, partly so it reflected our faith and sense of dependence in God, partly to reflect the vulnerability of many of the guests who came in such need, but also to prevent it becoming too institutional and losing its soul.

John McClauslen, a former chair of the trustees of Pilsdon, understood this well. In an introduction to its fortieth anniversary brochure, he wrote:

> Life at Pilsdon is simple, so that everyone can share it without the divisions and anxieties that acquisitive materialism may bring. But it is a precious thing to meet real needs – for food, shelter, comfort, health and peace – and to meet them well; the daily routine of necessary work to that end offers dignity for everyone. (McClauslen 1998)

Knowing our need of others, and responding to those in need, keep a community honest and vital, but knowing when to set limits on how much the community could do for people, and keeping people safe and well resourced was also crucial to its health. 'Sustainable vulnerability' seemed to sum up this tender balance – learning a way of being with people in their real need without being overwhelmed by it. In community, we accompany others well when we are aware of our own needs, and thus are less likely to be worn out by unconsciously seeking to meet our own needs through trying to help others. Accompaniment in community and in general isn't about helping people, but rather being alongside others in a way that allows them to find a sense of acceptance and belonging that gives them the space to find what they need.

CELEBRATION

The Pilsdon Community was full of sorrow, but it was a sorrow that was held and shared and would often give way to a deep sense of joy once people realised that their past suffering was also known and shared by others. This deep sense of belonging that people felt was expressed through our common work and communal celebrations. Each year at Pilsdon was given structure and rhythm through a whole series of community events. In January, clearing the manure from the cows' winter quarters would be the first major work demanding the participation of the whole community. Shrove Tuesday or Pancake Day, usually in February, would be marked by the annual wheelbarrow race around the courtyard, with several relay teams pushing the smallest team member in a wheelbarrow, clinging onto a frying pan and pancake, and seeking to avoid various obstacles around a hilarious circuit. At Easter, a huge tomb would be built at the back of the church, with a millstone rolling open to show the empty tomb. Soon after, people would line up along the fence to watch the cows joyfully kicking up their heels, cavorting in the fields as they were let out onto fresh grass after the winter. Which meant, of course, more communal cleaning of their winter area. Summer brought everyone out into the fields for haymaking. Autumn brought the 'Anniversary', which was a huge open day commemorating the founding of the community, and great effort was put into cleaning the house and gardens and preparing food for 200-plus visitors. Winter brought woodcutting, collecting and splitting, and huge open fires in the house for Christmas. The pattern of the year brought a familiar kind of comfort to people, and common work and celebration seemed to bind people together in a kind of living tradition.

In contrast, the 'commercial year', as played out in shop windows and in TV and other advertising media, seems to me much more formulaic and lacking in authenticity. The year begins with the chance to sell products to help people stop smoking, lose weight or achieve the perfect body shape that none of us has. It then moves on to Valentine's Day, seeing the opportunity for restaurants, hotels, chocolatiers and florists to boost sales. Then we have Mother's Day, reminding us to show how much we think our mums are worth. Then further sales for Easter. If it's a World Cup year, there's an excuse to drink more beer whilst watching your new extra-widescreen TV, then Halloween and the mega-bucks Christmas fest.

Call me cynical, but I'd much rather be pushing a wheelbarrow full of shit down the farmyard than rushing round a shopping centre looking for that perfect gift.

At Hilfield Friary, the year begins with the season of Advent, a time of waiting and reflection, and the first Christmas carol isn't sung until Midnight Mass. The twelve days of Christmas are fully celebrated, and it's a relief to get back to the pattern of work on the seventh of January. The celebration of Burns Night, to honour our Scottish guests or those with Scots antecedents, then follows, with the ceremonial slaying of the haggis after it has been piped in. If we have community members from the USA, we also celebrate Thanksgiving. When we are blessed with Chinese visitors, we honour the Chinese New Year. Easter begins with a great fire in the cemetery at dawn, on Ascension Day we sing hymns on the roof of the main house as the swallows swoop around us. In late June, in a spell of hot weather, we'll be out in the fields harvesting hay. In July we give thanks for our neighbours, with a barbecue for the local community and friends of the friary, for which one of our young cattle will be slaughtered. Cider pressed from our autumn apples will be put away for next year's haymaking. In October we celebrate the Feast of St Francis, with a couple of days of preparation and liturgy in the church, followed by a celebratory meal in our big dining hall. It sometimes feels like we're living in medieval England, with our lives framed by the rhythms of the church's year and the agricultural cycle.

The great value of common celebration seems to be how it binds people together and builds and tells a shared story. Photographing and sharing the story on social media also seems to be a way of reinforcing the joy and value of the common event. In the depths of winter at Pilsdon, on a bitterly cold morning, there was nothing more heartening than splitting open a bale of hay and finding in front of you a pressed summer flower as, nosing the hay, you recalled the warmth and sweet smell of summer, knowing it would come again. Likewise, documenting celebration is also a reminder of past joy and an affirmation of our common bonds and that we are in an ongoing cycle of belonging. On the Beechdale estate, where I worked as a local vicar, we did a lot of arts projects and eventually had an annual cycle of events, all of which sought to celebrate positive stories in the community. The year would begin with a big community pantomime, involving weeks of rehearsal and costume and set design, the summer would be marked by a week-long arts festival showcasing local talent in various venues across the estate, and the year would end with a 200-strong lantern procession and Christmas variety show. After each event we would always have an evaluation and celebration, which would involve showing photographs or a film of the event, a brief discussion of how we might do things better, followed by food or a party. These celebrations were crucial in affirming the projects and people's contribution to them, and reminded people of the capacity of artistic celebration to strengthen the bonds of community. A good celebration creates community memories, publicly defines the community, and fosters a sense of belonging.

Community celebrations are a public expression of what the notion of accompaniment asserts: that we belong together and are strengthened as individuals by being together. If the fundamental malaise of our society is loneliness, isolation and separation, then the solution to this is learning how to be with others again and learning to accompany others.

My first year living in community at Pilsdon was boisterous and joyous, as I adjusted to life in a vibrant, diverse community, welcoming a rich variety of often very needy people, and I began to realise that if I didn't find a sustainable way of being with others in community, I was in danger of burnout. In his book *A Cry Is Heard* (Vanier and Maigre 2018), Jean Vanier writes how burnout is an illness of the generous, and how in 1976 he spent two months in a hospital bed after exhausting himself caring for others. This was a turning point for him, as he was then forced to adjust his way of living in community from being a carer who just kept giving to someone who learnt to also receive from the people with learning disabilities he lived with. He writes that it's vital that those engaged in the care of others see it as a reciprocal relationship:

They do a lot for others, they give, but they don't always know how to receive. People who are generous must learn how to stop, in order to welcome the joy of the encounter and communion with the other, and agree to be transformed by the one they are caring for. Like I needed to do. The hospital helped me to be more free. (Vanier and Maigre 2018, p.63)

Towards the end of my first year at Pilsdon, I began to evolve a way of being with people that I would much later be able to name as accompaniment, which allowed me not only to survive in community but also to discover a real sense of joy and freedom that can come through a mutual sense of interdependence. I stopped trying to help people or change them, I began to let go of my need to be needed by others and to realise that the simple joy of being with others, accepting them for who they were and being as much aware of my own weaknesses as theirs, brought me a sense of real freedom, built community and fostered belonging. Developing and nurturing within myself generosity, humility, trust and knowing my own need of others was all part of a hidden process that taught me how to be with others. It wasn't till I left Pilsdon and went on pilgrimage to Santiago de Compostela that I began to reflect further on this way of being with others and name it accompaniment.

3

WALKING ALONGSIDE OTHERS

I'm sitting on a straw bale in the middle of the simple medieval church at the Pilsdon Community. I'm surrounded by members of the community and friends I've built up over my years here, and there's a low hum of a pair of hair clippers, as my head is ritually shaved. As my hair falls on the stone floor, I begin to feel a deep sense of loss for the community I'll be leaving. I tell people that in a number of cultures the shaving of heads is a mourning ritual, the outer loss of hair mirroring an inner sense of grief. The regrowth of hair also symbolises the possibility of new life. Pilgrims in many faith traditions, such as Islam and Hinduism, also shave their heads to mark the start of a pilgrimage, and I'm about to go on one.

On the flagstones, in the middle of the church, are my backpack and a staff. I kneel for a final blessing then pick up my pack and, for the first and only time, hoisting the rucksack onto my back feels light and easy, as, paradoxically, my picking it up represents laying down the burden of the leadership of the community, which has weighed heavy on me for the past five years. I'm holding on to so much emotion, tearing myself away from people and a way of living I've loved and so deeply identified with. The fear about what the future might hold. A sense of guilt about abandoning my fellow community members who have been such loyal and supportive colleagues. But also a great sense of elation, a feeling of great freedom, the letting go of responsibility for a while, and a sense of adventure. I also pick up a stout five-foot hazel staff I've cut from the hedgerow and the grip of it immediately feels comforting. It'll be my constant companion for over 500 miles, give physical support, make me look and feel like a pilgrim, and be a symbol of accompaniment. At the door to the porch of the church, I turn to face my companions for the last time, smiling through tears. I dramatically bang the stick on the ground, silently wave, turn, open the door and begin walking on a new journey to Santiago de Compostela.

I'd long been attracted to the idea of going on pilgrimage, and the idea of the sense of freedom and joy in travelling to a destination with others, sharing the highs and lows of a journey, suspending time, stepping out of the ordinary, going on an adventure. I've always enjoyed the rhythm you get into on a long walk, passing through a landscape, slowly becoming part of it, but most of all, I think, I enjoy the depth of conversation that can unfold as you walk alongside someone else. I was also attracted to the simplicity and egalitarian nature of going on a walk together. On a pilgrimage, everyone treads the same route and shares the same simple accommodation; all get tired, all need the encouragement of others, and carrying your own pack means that everyone travels light.

Too often in our society, there's a lack of connection with others; individuals feel increasingly lonely, whole groups of people are pushed to the margins, and it seems that we've forgotten that simplest, yet essential, human virtue of being with someone else. At Pilsdon, I'd learnt how deadly loneliness could be, but how, through community life and being with others, people's lives could be restored. Going on pilgrimage, as well as giving me the space to work out what I wanted to do next, was also a chance to explore how walking alongside others felt. What appealed most to me about the idea of going on pilgrimage was the inevitability of having to mix and be with a wide variety of people from many different cultures and share a walk together.

I wanted to walk with a sense of freedom and joy and in this I was helped by a conversation I'd had with my friend Viv, as we were planning a weekend focusing on pilgrimage as an outer and an inner journey. We planned that we'd walk to the shrine of St Witte at Whitchurch Canonicorum, a major centre of pilgrimage in Dorset in the Middle Ages. On the way to the church of St Witte, I told Viv there was a pub on a crossroads called the Shaves Cross Inn with a picture of a pilgrim having his head shaved on the pub sign. I said that I liked the idea of head shaving as a ritual sign of penitence, but that local historians thought the inn misnamed and it should really be called Shrives Cross. This was to do with the word 'shriven', which is an old English word for a priest absolving a penitent of all their sins. This would make more sense, as surely the pilgrim would have had their head shaved at the beginning of the journey rather than three miles from the shrine. Viv looked up the origins of the word 'shrive' and came across the associated phrase to be 'given short shrift'; today it means to be quickly dismissive of someone, but it comes from the short walk a condemned prisoner would take, following their final confession to a priest, in the final moments before execution. Viv took it to mean it was a walk of total freedom, as the person, absolved of their sins, had no time to sin again before their death and meeting with God. I resolved to try and walk with this sense of freedom, to walk as if each day was the last or only day of my life, to receive each day as a gift, to try, wherever possible, to stay in the moment. Leaving the past behind, not wasting energy worrying about the future, just putting one step in front of the other. To, as they say in Alcoholics Anonymous, 'keep it in the day'.

LONELINESS

Having arrived in Spain, my first few days were full of this joy, setting off each morning with nothing to think about but the open road. I had no guidebook, all I had was an A4 sheet of paper with the distances between Pilgrim hostels and cheap places to stay on the way. So I set off each day with the rough intention of where I might stop over each night, but if I felt tired or liked the look of a place, I might finish early or, if I wanted to, go further. All I needed to do was walk and stay in the moment; it felt like a wonderful freedom.

I decided to walk alone in the daytime, enjoying the solitude, but be gregarious in the evenings.

Sometimes it would happen, though, that I'd fall into conversation with someone on the road and we might talk in depth for a couple of hours, then I'd return to my solitary rhythm. The first few days were rich and full of a wonderful lightness and openness, but, my first couple of evenings I felt lonely and excluded. I didn't manage to engage with anyone, people seemed to be in national groups, speaking their own languages, and I had a miserable couple of meals eating on my own. I, who was used to eating with at least 30 other people, was no longer part of a community, but alone. I, who had rejected the growing individualism of contemporary Western society in favour of living communally, now felt dismally alone.

Loneliness is one of the great blights of British society, with increasing numbers of people, particularly men, living alone. An ever-mobile population, the increase in family breakdown, greater longevity, and a culture that vigorously promotes individual autonomy are all contributing to an epidemic of loneliness. In 2019, 7.7 million people live in single households, a figure that has increased by 16 per cent over the past 20 years (Office for National Statistics 2019). Recent research shows that someone who is chronically lonely is likely to live seven years less than someone with good social connections. Margaret Bolton, researching for Oxford Age UK, writes that loneliness has an equivalent effect on the body as smoking 15 cigarettes a day. Loneliness leads to a reduced level of cortisol, which fights inflammation, breaks down fats and sugars, and gives you energy. A lack of cortisol also inhibits healthy working of the immune system. Loneliness negatively affects people's mental health; whilst depression affects one in five people living in a community, it affects two in five living in care homes (Bolton 2012).

I know from personal experience that loneliness is a killer. A number of people who left the Pilsdon Community and moved into their own flats and independence were dead within a few months, having succumbed, once more, to alcoholism and drunk themselves to death, or fallen into a depression so deep it led to them taking their own lives. As the Campaign to End Loneliness so rightly says, 'Loneliness is a killer.'

The solitude I experienced walking in the day didn't feel like loneliness. It felt like an intentional separation from others, which made me more attentive to the natural world around me and my own feelings. Being on my own in the evenings, though, definitely felt like alienation, and I was determined not to become isolated and lonely. I had a simple strategy that revolved around food, that great bringer-together of people. I would invite others to eat with me or invite myself to eat with others. Sometimes this would mean going out together to a bar to eat, other times it meant me cooking for others or sharing in the cooking with others. It worked beautifully. I never ate alone again and met so many different people. The word 'companion' comes from 'panis', the Latin for bread, and was originally used to describe someone with whom you shared a meal. The food we made and ate together was simple fare, but the act of preparing and sharing it bound us together as, of course, did our common walk.

I experienced a deep sense of companionship on the road, often silently watching groups of people, couples and individuals stretched out ahead of me as the road rose or fell before me. The simple and joyful pilgrimage greeting of 'Bon Camino!' from fellow walkers and locals, as we passed each other, bound us together.

I always stayed at the cheapest places, called 'refugios', and life in these was good and simple. A place to leave your boots, a bar of soap and a big sink to handwash clothes, some kind of toilet and shower, and a communal dormitory. I was a little surprised to find men and women sharing the same sleeping places but soon got used to it. The common spirit of the Camino seemed to break down notions of segregation and threat and build trust between us.

The most profound conversations, of course, happened in those one-to-one conversations I allowed myself to have when I intuitively felt the need to talk or listen to another. This took companionship to the associated but deeper level of what I would call accompaniment. Maybe it was the freedom of the road which encouraged people to open up to each other, perhaps it was because so many people were inhabiting the liminal space I was also in, maybe it was because our meetings were transient and we might never see the person again; many conversations quickly reached a depth and honesty that doesn't come quickly in the midst of daily life. It felt a bit like being back at Pilsdon where, because so many people there were living with a lot of pain and brokenness and often in the liminal space of recovery, there tended to be a culture of openness and lack of judgement.

ENTERING LIMINAL SPACE

When I arrived in Spain, one of the few bits of Spanish I had learnt was 'Dondo est Camino?', literally 'Where is the way?' or 'Where's the footpath?', which I thought would be very useful. In the end, though, I found that the route I began to walk was so well marked and well trodden, you'd have to be a complete fool or totally lost in conversation or self-absorption to miss it. So I never asked the question, though I did think it was a question I needed to begin asking myself. 'Where am I going?' 'What's next?' But I also intuitively knew it wasn't really a question for the pilgrimage, which for me needed to be more about transition, a space between leaving the place I so loved and moving on to whatever was next.

Many others walking the 'Camino' were also in that in-between space, the neither here nor there, but rather betwixt and between. The place social anthropologists call liminal. In Latin, the 'limen' was the raised bit of ground below the front door, which prevented mud and water from flowing into the house – what we, today, would call the threshold. I felt like I was standing in the doorway, not sure whether I was coming or going, to use another much-used phrase. So many others walking were doing so because they also had entered this liminal space. There were the newly bereaved, those recently divorced, people who'd been made redundant, people in-between jobs, those taking sabbaticals. There seemed to be more people making the pilgrimage for this reason than there were pilgrims walking for religious reasons or those who loved long-distance footpaths.

In the 2011 film *The Way*, Michael Sheen plays a father whose son Daniel was struck by lightning as he began the Camino in the Pyrenees. The film is about the father beginning to work through his grief, as he decides to walk to Compostela in the place of his son. He walks with a group of three others who all carry their own hurts and grief, which begin to be worked out over the course of the walk.

Going on pilgrimage, for me, was a walking into liminal space, being prepared to step into that place of not knowing, the place where things are beyond our control, a place of waiting, a place of transition. All societies used to have rites of passage to help people negotiate these liminal times, which are full of uncertainty: rituals around birth, puberty, marriage, death and other times of momentous change which helped individuals and the community make sense of and articulate their fears, and be with one another in solidarity in times of grief and change. In the West, as corporate solidarity has been slowly eroded, the decline in religious and secular ritual has led to a further dissolution of the bonds between us. It's now becoming increasingly popular to have a memorial service without a body, which will already have quietly been disposed of at the crematorium. However well crafted the memorial service, it will inevitably, somehow, be once removed from the reality of having the body of the deceased present, and though on one level it spares the relatives the discomfort of watching their loved one go into the ground or behind the curtain into the incinerator, I think there's a missed opportunity to share grief together.

In contrast to this, my experience of Gypsy funerals is that they are an opportunity for intense outpourings of grief. The extended family will have been sitting up drinking tea all night, with the body in an open coffin, and on the day of the funeral everyone related to the deceased will turn out, often in their hundreds, in a huge show of solidarity. Floral tributes will be sat on the back of flatbed trucks and at the graveside a vast scrum of people will gather, with much wailing and weeping as the coffin is lowered into the ground, and then the men will quickly fill in the grave. Then all will gather for the wake. In the Traveller community, that huge gap that opens up when someone dies is both acknowledged and ameliorated by the accompaniment of the whole community at the time of crisis.

Walking alongside others on the Camino for many was also, I think, a way of coming to terms with loss.

WALKING TOGETHER

Walking alongside another, sharing the same road, opens us up to one another. Some months after completing the Camino, I joined the World Council of Churches Ecumenical Accompaniment Programme in Palestine and Israel (EAPPI), and I immediately connected with the name and the notion of accompaniment. This walking alongside others seemed a profoundly human and liberating thing to do. In the training for the programme, I met a Swedish woman, Brigit, who was a radio journalist. As we walked through East Jerusalem one evening, she told me she had broken her back when she fell off a roof some years ago. In hospital, she was told she might never walk again, and she resolved that, should she learn to walk again, she would never refuse the offer to go for a walk if asked, however tired and reluctant she felt. After hearing Brigit's story, I've also resolved never to turn down the invitation of a walk, and sometimes, if someone wants to talk to me or I need to talk something through, I'll suggest we go for a walk together. I try and keep in mind the Native American saying 'Never judge another till you've walked a mile in their moccasins.' There's something about walking with someone that feels freeing, feels highly egalitarian, and helps break down difference and puts us in a wider, more expansive context. Like going on pilgrimage, it's an outward sign of an inner journey, and it's also a sign of solidarity with others. Walking is what we were built for once our ancestors came down from the trees, and it feels like the right speed to be moving. Travelling in a car after a day walking, it's always a shock to me just how quickly the landscape rushes past and how my stress level seems to rise.

Some of my Traveller friends who still live in a bow top wagon, drawn by a horse, speak of the madness of rushing round in a car, though, of course, they're seen as the strangely different ones. A horse and wagon covers about the same distance in a day as a person walking, averaging about 15 miles a day. This sort of pace gives time to take in and be part of the landscape and feel a greater sense of belonging to the earth, on which we all walk. I've often found that when trying to think through a difficult issue, taking a walk has led me towards a solution to the particular problem. Working things out and processing difficult feelings was certainly something I was doing with countless others as we followed the Camino to Compostela.

In the New Testament there's a famous story where, on the road to Emmaus, a small town outside Jerusalem, two men who were followers of the prophet Jesus meet a stranger. They tell him of the execution of their leader, Jesus, and how their hopes that he was to be the Messiah, the one to lead them out from Roman oppression, have been dashed by his death. As they walk, they share their grief and lost hopes and listen as the stranger tells them that their tradition tells of how the Messiah would suffer and die but be raised again. As they journey on, they feel a sense of new hope stirring in them and urge the stranger to stay with them and share food. As the stranger breaks bread with them, they suddenly realise it's Jesus returned from the dead, and he then leaves them. In the story it says, in some translations, 'it was as if scales fell from their eyes'. In his painting The Supper at Emmaus, Caravaggio, through his use of light, captures this moment of amazed realisation.

Walking alone and walking with others definitely can allow things to shift in our understanding and fresh insight can be gifted. As I moved along the road and shared my story with others, I felt things slowly begin to shift internally. The story of the Road to Emmaus and the idea of accompaniment represented in it kept replaying itself in my mind. I loved this idea that the purpose of our lives was not to strive to be successful and constantly achieve more status, power and wealth, but rather to walk alongside others. This was the way I'd unconsciously chosen and been affirmed in by others, and now I had this image of accompaniment to make sense of my journey in life. The story of the Road to Emmaus and the notion of accompaniment seem to tell me that if I lapse into despair, or fail to process my own grief and cut myself off from others, I'll remain isolated and divided from others. If, though, I choose to welcome the stranger, listen to what they might be telling me, offer time and hospitality to the other, then something quite unexpected and life-giving is always likely to happen.

Satish Kumar, former Jain monk, environmentalist and editor of *Resurgence & Ecologist* magazine, writes in it of the healing power of walking (Kumar 2016). He writes how environmental and political activists such as Gandhi in his Salt March or Martin Luther King through his march to Washington, where he delivered his 'I Have a Dream' speech, have used walking as not only acts of political defiance but spiritual awakening. In 1965, at the height of the Cold War, Kumar started out on a peace walk from New Delhi to Moscow, Paris, London and Washington. He set off without a penny in his pocket and others joined him along the 8000 miles he walked in total. He says he may not have brought about world peace but he did find peace within himself. He is now 83 and still walks for an hour each day.

> People ask me, what is the secret of your good health? My answer is plain and simple, I just use one word, 'walking'. It is good for my body, good for my mind and good for my spirit. I walk for an hour or so each day. No words are sufficient to contain my praise for walking. I choose to move and flow rather than to remain static. (Kumar 2016)

Satish Kumar said that, as a result of his peace walk, he learnt to trust and depend on strangers, drop his fear of the unknown and unplanned, and come to deeply love the landscapes through which he passed. He learnt to accept hospitality and hostility, good weather and bad with equanimity.

Two Buddhist monks from a Thai order based in Devon recently stayed over at Hilfield Friary on a walking pilgrimage they were making. Like Satish Kumar, they set off with nothing other than their saffron robes, a pair of sandals and a begging bowl. I was cooking that day, and was delighted to fill up their stainless steel bowls with curry and rice, fetch them water, drag a bench into the shade of a tree and leave them to eat in silence. Later on, I fell into conversation with the younger monk about why they were off wandering. He said it was part of their tradition to go travelling and depend on the kindness of strangers. He went on to say that something very spiritually warm happens when you stretch out your bowl for food and someone fills it. Choosing to beg makes you vulnerable and, usually, brings out the generosity of others, but also evokes a deep sense of gratitude in the one who's asked for food. He said, 'It's as though, as the bowl fills up with food, so I fill up with an overwhelming sense of gratitude.' They stayed a night, had breakfast, and before they left, I asked if they wanted me to make them sandwiches, guessing what the answer would be; I was right, they chose to travel light.

In February 2016, I was walking down a road in Calais to the infamous Jungle, a makeshift refugee camp on the old town dump, with Brother Johannes, another monk from the Old Catholic Church. Brother Johannes, inspired by his contact with the Catholic Worker movement, felt called to set up a house of prayer and hospitality in the town. As we walked alongside each other for the couple of miles to the camp, I shared this idea of accompaniment with him and realised, as we walked, that this was exactly what he was living out. Around midday, he'd walk to the camp and, on the way, stop and meet refugees, often walking back with individuals who were returning from failed attempts to climb aboard lorries bound for Dover. As they walked, they'd tell him their story.

As we arrived in the camp, I was struck by Brother Johannes' approach. Instead of going to dispense charity by working in a soup kitchen, or handing out shoes and clothing, or going to teach English, or organising games with the children, we simply walked amongst the people. He'd greet people he knew, stop for tea in one of the makeshift cafés, constructed from pallets and plastic sheeting, and simply be amongst people. Volunteers in the camp with great energy and imagination were running a huge array of charitable projects:

schools, a legal advice centre, a theatre for unaccompanied children, cricket coaching and much more. Many volunteers had given up time, and some had given up jobs, to help these dispossessed people, and I felt that their commitment to the cause was something akin to that of those who joined the International Brigades to fight fascism in Spain in 1936. This was all hugely impressive but contrasted with Johannes' approach, which was simply to be with the people. He wasn't just quietly supporting the refugees but also the dozens of often highly stressed volunteers, some traumatised by the horrific stories migrants shared with them. As others rushed about, stirring huge cauldrons of food, crowd-controlling people not queuing up properly for the daily clothes handout, Johannes, in his faded blue monk's habit, simply walked and sat amongst the people. The camp too was a liminal space, many refugees waiting there months and sometimes years, caught between the journey from their homeland and the promised land of the UK, 20 miles across the Channel. The Jungle was very much a temporary place, a stopping place on the way; it was a place of waiting and Johannes' way of simply being with people seemed to mirror this.

I stood around too, sometimes feeling helpless and useless, feeling the desire to go and chop onions and do something useful amidst all this need and human suffering, but I knew, from my experience working with Gypsies, that if you can bear to wait, just hang around, an important conversation, that real meeting with someone, can happen. It's again about being prepared to step into that empty space, the neither here nor there, the place of undefined role. It's scary, uncomfortable, but can turn into a place of real encounter. Doing nothing, being nothing, achieving nothing, but making space for the other. Sure enough, people began to talk to me and told me of being forced to flee, their journeys, separation from families, their longing to return one day to their homeland, but in the meantime their hope of reaching friends and family in the UK. They too were living in liminal space betwixt and between.

After a few hours, it was time to walk back to the house, which we did in silence. This helped me process some of the stories I'd heard, things I'd seen and feelings evoked. Once back at the house, there was tea and cake around a common table and then simple prayers in the chapel, which doubled up as an emergency bedroom for some of the most vulnerable in the camp. The next day, there was morning prayer then the walk again to the camp, and more hanging around.

ACCOMPANIMENT

This ability, this calling of Brother Johannes to accompany others and simply walk alongside them, connected deeply with me. His willingness to step into the Jungle and just be there epitomised, to me, what was at the heart of the notion of accompaniment. Something unquantifiable, hard to measure, but at the heart of what it means to be human. Good accompaniment, I think, helps us navigate the uncertainty of liminal space and can give us the courage to stay in a place of not knowing and transition rather than jumping onto the next available train out of town.

Physically, Johannes bore similarities to a former mentor of mine, the Reverend Jim Garnett, who had trained me in my first three years as a newly ordained priest. Like Johannes, Jim had gingery, curly hair, a ruddy complexion and a smile that came mostly from his eyes. Like Johannes, he chose to walk alongside those in need without judgement and without the compulsion to try and fix things for them. I ended up working with him almost by accident.

When looking for my first job, I'd been told that the most important thing was not the place, but my relationship with what was called my training incumbent. I went to look at an inner-city parish in Birmingham, which seemed the perfect place for me. Next door to the church was a mosque, at the end of the road was a gurdwara and two streets away was a Hindu temple, just the kind of multifaith environment I wanted to immerse myself in. At the church, the worship was vibrant yet devotional, the congregation 80 per cent black with the singing of a full gospel choir lifting me onto another plane. I knew, though, that I wasn't going there as after ten minutes in the company of the vicar, I knew we'd never get on. He was an activist and, as soon as he opened the door to me, he said, as if to test me, 'You can come in for a cup of tea or we can go and walk around the parish.' I chose the walk, which was at speed, included a number of rushed visits to parishioners and came with a cascade of information about the local area. He never asked me anything about myself, but described, in detail, the role he expected me to play. It felt like the perfect place to be, but I sensed there'd be a lot more rushing round doing things rather than being with people, and I knew I'd struggle to work with him.

In contrast, for my interview with Jim we went to the Pingwood, a rough pub on Tower Hill, a run-down 1970s council estate with no cultural diversity. The locals used to call the estate 'Beirut', because of the number of burnt-out and empty buildings and wrecks of cars that had been stolen, brought back to the estate at high speed and then set on fire. St Andrews Church had been built to be vandal proof, with sheet steel doors, no windows, only clear fibreglass sheets high up to let light in and the drainpipes on the inside of the building. At the end of the 1980s, adult unemployment on the estate ran at 35 per cent and youth unemployment at 80 per cent. It felt like an abandoned place, but my intuition told me to go there and be with Jim.

Like Johannes, Jim had no strategy or plans for his parish, beyond simply walking alongside the people there. As we sat in the pub, shouting at one another over the jukebox, he asked me a little about myself and introduced me to the locals. Several pints later, as we left at closing time, I knew I had passed Jim's only test, as I'd felt comfortable and at home in one of the few meeting places on Tower Hill.

For my first six weeks in the job, I kept waiting for Jim to tell me what to do and where to go and what to put in my diary. That, though, wasn't his style, and when I asked him what he thought I should be doing, and when we were going to have a mentoring session, he replied that if I listened to the people of Tower Hill and immersed myself in the life here, they'd be the ones to train me and their compassion and support for one another would teach me plenty about Christianity. 'Besides,' he laughed, 'haven't you noticed, we've been having our mentoring sessions in the Pear Tree after the five-a-side football we play on a Friday evening!'

I, of course, learnt a huge amount from being with him and watching how he was with others. I remember him saying at the funeral of Edie, who'd been one of the faithful members of our small church congregation, 'I'm glad she walked this way,' and it was this ability to walk alongside people with love and without judgement that I most appreciated in Jim. Whenever we were asked to take a funeral on Tower Hill, there tended to be an element of tragedy in it, because the population of Tower Hill was predominately made up of young families. On hearing of a death, we would visit the families on several occasions before the funeral itself, where we would share stories about the deceased, but also just share time with them. Inevitably in that community, we would sit up drinking with them, and I remember one night in summer not leaving the house until daylight.

When the day of the funeral dawned, this time spent with the families meant that Jim could make the service more intimate and personal – maybe he hadn't known the deceased, but he'd come to know and be known as part of the bereaved family. One funeral Jim took was of a young man called Peter, killed in a motorbike crash. He began his address in tears, saying, 'I also have a son called Peter, he's also 26 years old, but, for some reason, he's alive and your boy is dead.' Another funeral he began by taking out a packet of cigarettes and pretending to offer them to the congregation, just reminding people of the hundreds of fags they'd smoked together in the nights before the funeral. Such empathy.

Jim was a breaker-down of walls between people, and he did it by gently being present, humbly listening to others without judgement, and asserting his primary belief, summed up in his favourite phrase, 'God's good.' He saw the good in everything and everyone and sought to communicate this simple truth to whoever would listen. He wasn't afraid to stand in that liminal space of not knowing, not having anything to offer other than himself and his faith in a God of love. He saw the dangers of people building walls around themselves and the dangers of what happens when we forget how to relate to one another. He saw how institutions could cut people off from one another and would often tell me that the opposite of love wasn't hate but fear. He was opposed to fundamentalism, in all its forms, and saw it as a response to fear and a lack of openness to others. Thirty years on, as I look at the growth of sectarianism and the desire for easy answers, and the delight people seem to have in taking offence at others with a different background, culture or views, I appreciate, more and more, Jim's simple honesty and his ability to get alongside others.

Of course, he wasn't perfect. He drank too much, was a poor organiser, and rarely attended meetings. The institutional church inevitably struggled with his unorthodox approach and finally he was forced to move on, but his deep humanity, lack of judgement and willingness to walk alongside people continues to shape and influence the way I try to be with people. I'm deeply grateful to have walked a while with Jim.

This gentle notion of accompaniment, I think, stands at the heart of what it means to be human, and countercultural as it may sometimes feel, is a fundamental building block of healthy communities and a compassionate society. Too often today, people don't listen to one another, rather we talk at one another, feeling the need to define ourselves by our opinions, rather than defining ourselves by our relationships with others. This urge to establish and defend our position, rather than bringing us security, instead can lead us to a place of loneliness and a superficial sense of belonging to others who share similar, well-defended positions. We signal our virtue by condemning others and dismissing and, perhaps, ridiculing their opinions in real and virtual conversations with others who share our views. This further entrenches us in our sense of superiority, whilst also distancing and separating ourselves from those with different views, who then become 'the others'. By taking offence at others, we are also able to control where our conflicts are. The thing that most effectively breaks this cycle of division is a willingness, even for a short time, to walk alongside the other and begin to listen to who they really are and come to know their story. I know that each time I really connect with someone who walks alongside me and really listens to me, I feel deeply met and much lighter and freer.

One of the challenges for me, living in rural Dorset for the past 24 years, with my passionate concern for social justice and love of diversity, has been living in a largely white and socially conservative community. When I have managed to build friendships with several farmers who have a very different world view, these have been some of my most precious relationships. Most of these farming friendships have grown through working together on joint projects, sharing water, equipment and our land, and through shared work, building trust. The unlikely nature of these friendships has made them all the more valuable, as we've had to work hard at them to overcome our different backgrounds, but, once built, they seem very solid, as we've transcended our inbuilt prejudices and preconceived ideas about one another. The thing that built the friendship was nearly always the working alongside each other combined with our listening to each other.

SPIRITUAL ACCOMPANIMENT

My mentor and spiritual director, Graham Chadwick, was someone who, through his skill at listening to others, effortlessly crossed cultural barriers. He was a great linguist and had been a missionary priest in Lesotho in Southern Africa, became a bishop there and then was appointed as Bishop of Kimberly in the Republic of South Africa at the height of Apartheid. He made himself deeply unpopular with the government by asking too many questions about leaders of the Black Consciousness movement, like Steve Biko, who had been dying in suspiciously large numbers whilst in police detention. He was banned from his diocese but, on Easter Sunday in 1980, he returned to Kimberley Cathedral to preach in English, Sotho and Afrikaans. He was arrested and issued with a deportation order. At the airport, over 50,000 Africans turned up to sing to mark his departure, such was the affection for him. Back in the UK, he became Bishop of St Asaph in North Wales where he teamed up with a Jesuit priest, Father

Gerry Hughes, who had begun a movement to make the teaching of spiritual direction and the training of people for it much more open and accessible. In fact, Graham and Gerry never talked about spiritual direction but rather began to call it spiritual accompaniment.

I came to know Graham by taking part in a two-week training course for spiritual accompaniers at Lys Fasi in North Wales. I was struck by his humility, earthiness and twinkling humour. One of my favourite phrases of his is, 'Christianity is more than a movement for people from the cradle to the grave, rather it should be from the erection to the resurrection.' The wisdom I quote most from him, though, is about the need to sometimes just hang around with people, being available for them with no fixed agenda. He told me that in the Sotho language there's no word for wasting time, only making time. He certainly made time for me over the years, and accompanied me, for a time, on my spiritual journey. Just as the pilgrimage to Compostela is an outer journey through the landscape of mountains and plains, so too, I believe, we are all called to make an inner journey. Writing about the sixteenth-century Spanish mystic Theresa of Avila, J. Welch (1982, p.37) says, 'Pilgrimage is extroverted mysticism and mysticism is introverted pilgrimage.'

As for the outer journey we need guides and signposts on the way, so for the inner journey we need people to point us in the right direction and help us discover the path we are called to walk. Graham was able to do this for me with great skill and a lightness of touch, occasionally prompting and challenging but most of the time just gently accompanying me. In the Christian tradition, this practice of being alongside others has been called spiritual direction and, at times, has been seen as the preserve of religious professionals, largely priests, who have often seen it as a teaching and training role, and, as the name implies, directive. This is mirrored in many Hindu traditions in the relationship between guru and disciple, and in Buddhism between the master and the seeker.

Graham's approach was very different, not based on passing on his rich store of wisdom but encouraging me to find my own way on this inner journey. He also never fell into the trap, like many religious professionals do, of taking himself too seriously. At his funeral, the story was told by the preacher of his arriving at Graham's house for a planning meeting for an important conference, and Graham greeting him at the door saying, 'Oh good, you're just in time for 'Allo 'Allo!' (a popular and farcical TV comedy). If the spiritual guide can pass on a sense of joy and the need to not take ourselves too seriously, it's a great gift and illustrates a real sense of inner freedom. The old-fashioned spiritual director, with a top-down instructive approach, would never have worked for me. I preferred the idea of someone offering a little guidance but mainly listening lovingly and accompanying me on my inner journey.

Today, there is a great revival in the churches of people seeking this spiritual accompaniment, which is also mirrored in the growth of those teaching mindfulness, yoga and meditation, the growing number of life coaches and the realisation of the importance of good one-to-one supervision for those with responsibility for others in industry and the public services. To have someone who'll make time to give you a really good listening-to is one of the most precious things in life, particularly when we're in a place of transition and not knowing. Good accompaniment can allow us to stay in that liminal space of not knowing, of apparent emptiness, and prevent us from falling back on the easy option of staying with the known and comfortable and never moving on.

The Celts had a saying, 'Anyone without a "soul friend" is like a body without a head.' To have someone who deeply listens to us and accompanies us on our inner journey can deepen and grow a sense of meaning and direction in our lives. To continue the analogy, without good accompaniment, we can run around like headless chickens.

In her book *Holy Listening* (1992), Margaret Guenther uses the image of midwife to describe the role of spiritual accompaniment. She sees the traditional term of spiritual director as too directive and limiting. The Orthodox Church has the tradition of people having a spiritual father who listens to the directee, whilst also giving clear guidance and direction in keeping with the teachings of the church. For her, this is a valid method but doesn't always lead to growth and maintains a parent–child relationship between director and directee. In contrast to this more patriarchal approach, Guenther uses this image of the accompanier as midwife: the one who sits with the pilgrim, supportive, attentive, listening, encouraging and only intervening when necessary, trusting that God knows best for them and that they'll usually find their way to new birth with skilled support rather than major intervention.

The great popularity in the UK of the television series *Call the Midwife* perhaps shows a hidden longing for and an appreciation of this gentle way of being with others. The religious sisters and midwives of St Nonnatus House, through their life of prayer and service to the impoverished population of 1950s Poplar in the East End of London, as well as instructing the secular midwives in the art of delivering babies, also model a life of compassion, based on being present in a community and treating all who come with love and without judgement. The few midwifes I've met seem to share a similar sense of compassion and this ability to patiently accompany people without needing to control and fix things. This way of working contrasts with so much modern medicine, which seems so focused on treating symptoms and disease without always taking time to be with and really listen to the patient.

Whilst living at Pilsdon, I helped deliver dozens of calves from our small herd of beautiful Jersey cows. We often artificially inseminated them with semen from a slightly larger breed of bull, which meant they frequently needed assistance when it came to calving. I learnt how to watch them carefully near the date they were due to calve. There'd be tell-tale signs a calving was imminent: the filling of the udders, signs of discomfort and restlessness, the cocking of the tail and, sometimes, a great gush as their waters broke. As I grew more experienced, I learnt to watch and wait rather than to rush to intervene. I'd go and sit down with a cup of tea and let events unfold in their own time. I remember the vet teaching on the calving course: 'The cow knows what to do, just watch and wait; as long as there's progression don't worry.' It's a lesson I apply in my spiritual accompaniment of others, namely that the person who's come to see you knows what they want to say and sometimes you just have to wait for it; and what they really need to say may take a bit of time to emerge. So often I hear people say to me, 'I don't know where to begin,' so I wait, and wait some more, letting the silence settle around us and then they usually begin where they need to.

With the calves I learnt to hold back and only intervene where necessary; sometimes a leg was bent and the calf had to be pushed back into the womb to straighten it, sometimes the cow got tired so I'd attach ropes to the front legs and head of the calf, smear generous amounts of lubrication and pull. Covered in dung, blood and amniotic fluid, I was always elated by each calving, the joy and magic of bringing new life into the world. Most of our guests at Pilsdon came from cities and many admitted to feeling emotionally stuck, so to see new life come wriggling into the world, in the shape of a newborn calf, provoked a sense of awe and wonder and symbolised the possibilities for them to let go of the past and move on to a kind of new birth.

Inspired by the work of Felicity Warner, a movement called Soul Midwives has been established to provide this kind of accompaniment and support for people who are dying, who are on what she calls the sacred threshold. Warner, in her book *Gentle Dying* (2008, p.2), says, 'A good death is an extraordinary, moving and sacred experience. It can also have a healing quality, not only for the person who is involved but their families, friends and wider community.'

Soul midwives provide an alternative to the medical model of dealing with death in most hospitals, where everything is done to keep the patient alive, busily using the best clinical methods and drugs available, dealing almost exclusively with the patient's physical needs, seeking to prolong life and ward off death. For so many, dying in hospital is efficient, clinical, functional and soulless, with many doctors having a sense of failure around death. In contrast, a Soul Midwife works not against the inevitability of death but with it, seeking to provide a sacred and a healing space for the dying person, usually in the comfort and dignity of their own home. They seek to accompany the dying one and their family and friends in that space between life and death. Their work seems to meet a need that would traditionally, in the UK, be met by the local priest, and it's an area that, as a priest, I still inhabit, being called to the bedside of the dying and arranging and leading funerals. I've always seen it as one of the most important parts of my calling, to be with people as they journey from this world to, I believe, the next and also to accompany the bereaved through their journey of grief. Grief too is a journey to be gone through and takes time. Where people seek to avoid it, through denial or overbusyness, it inevitably resurfaces in unhealthy ways, often manifesting itself in poor physical and mental health. To support people through it takes time and compassion, and a gentle walking alongside, letting each person's particular journey unfold.

It was grief I was carrying as I walked along the road to Compostela. In the film *The Way*, the bereaved father, played by Michael Sheen, is carrying his son's ashes, which he slowly distributes at significant places along the way. As I walked and talked to people along the way, I gradually began to lose some of the sense of loss I felt in leaving Pilsdon. Two days from arrival in Compostela, I missed a turning and ended up walking far longer than I intended, deep into the evening, and I arrived a day early on the hill overlooking the city. I sat and watched the sun go down over the twin spires of the cathedral and, for the first time, burst into an uncontrollable, shaking bout of tears. 'What are they about?' I thought. 'Tears of relief?' 'Tears of joy at reaching the end of the pilgrimage?' I thought about it a bit, then realised it was my grief at leaving Pilsdon coming out. I thought back to the old sister who'd persuaded me to enter the liminal space of pilgrimage to help me cope with the transition between leaving the community and whatever was next, and I was glad I'd listened to her.

A week later, I began life at Hilfield Friary. It was a lovely place but it didn't feel like coming home, which was how I felt the first day I walked into Pilsdon. My stay there was to be temporary; I knew I had a lot of inner work to do and would have to put up with a lot more not knowing. It felt like I was entering another liminal place of not knowing, a bit like one of those newborn calves. This felt really uncomfortable, so I returned to what I knew worked best for me, work with my hands. I knew that if I lost myself in the moment, working on the land, building things, fixing stuff, it would help assuage the grief I was still feeling and let me gently work through it, so that's what I turned to.

4

WORKING ALONGSIDE OTHERS

I'm toiling in a vineyard in the hot Italian sun at the foot of the hill that the city of Assisi is built on. I'm working between the rows of hard-pruned vines on land owned by the Bose Monastery, and my job is to pick up the tangled piles of prunings. It doesn't sound like much of a job but the brothers' tiny tractor has broken down so, for now, each bundle of sticks has to be wheelbarrowed by hand uphill to the bonfire site. I'm sweating hard, I didn't expect I'd need a hat in March and the sun is getting to my balding pate. My knees ache, my back is sore and I'm feeling my age. 'Why? Oh why did I volunteer so enthusiastically again for such backbreaking work?' I berate myself. Then I look up and see the city above me gleaming, with its pink and cream stone framed by a clear blue Mediterranean sky, and I look ahead of me over the plain and see the snow-capped Apennine Mountains in the distance and think, 'Maybe it's not such a bad place for a bit of good honest graft.'

The reason I'm working here is to get to know the Bose Community by working alongside them for a couple of weeks. My experience of living in community tells me that working alongside people, particularly in physically demanding tasks, builds trust and friendship better than almost anything else. The guests I generally get to know best at Hilfield Friary are the ones who join me in manual tasks. It's amazing how an afternoon of splitting logs can allow people to bond. I'd been having lunch with the Bose brothers the previous week and the conversation had been good, sharing common ground in our experiences of community life, but when one of the brothers was telling me how behind they were on pruning the olive groves and clearing the vine prunings, I had seized my chance and volunteered my labour.

Later, Brother Mikela comes back with the newly repaired tractor, which he calls 'Armageddon'. As the tractor reverses down the rows, with a deafening clanking, I fork the vine prunings onto the back of the trailer as it chugs remorselessly towards me. If I stop, I'm in danger of being run over and there's no way Mikela is going to hear me over the clanking engine, so I just have to work faster. Once everything's loaded, I jump into the front of the tiny cab next to this powerfully built and heavily bearded monk. Above the din he shouts at me, 'Jonathan, you're an angel, I never thought we'd finish this job!' Only an Italian would call another man an angel, and it delights me. I later learn from someone else that Mikela has said of me, 'That Jonathan, he works like a monk.' A compliment indeed.

More days of toil pass in the vineyard and then it's time for a final feast with, of course, wine from last year's vintage, and, as I leave, Mikela embraces me and kisses me on both cheeks and I know that, through our common experience of work, we have become brothers.

WORKING TOGETHER CONNECTS US AND GIVES PURPOSE

I feel lucky to have had the opportunity of working with my hands and accompanying people like Mikela in lots of manual work over the years. Though Mikela and I spoke little of each other's language, through working together we came to know and trust each other in a very real way. For most people in twenty-first-century Britain, work is often a solitary activity, involving a computer screen, in an office, sitting in a vehicle, or inside a building. We've contracted out most manual work to other nations, and even in 'hands-on' work, like farming, the tiny proportion of people now working the land are heavily dependent on machinery. So much work people are asked to do now seems to have little purpose, and the sole aim of engaging in work is to earn money in order to survive, so for many there is little joy in it. There's just something about the honesty and simplicity of physical work that binds people together, with a common sense of purpose that so often forges friendship. The loss of manual work is part of our disconnection from each other and can lead to a sense of purposelessness. Working with Mikela, who moved around the monastery land with energy and conviction, I couldn't help but be attracted by his enthusiasm for tasks many in our world would shun as belonging to the uneducated or unskilled. He also understood how simple manual work connects us.

Where work is repetitive and dull, this building of friendship is even more important. Where work is dangerous, perhaps that's when the strongest bonds of trust and solidarity are built. Tudor Botwood, who is a chaplain in the Royal Marines and did several tours of Afghanistan, says that the bonds of friendship forged whilst out on patrol in such a dangerous place are hard to replicate in civilian life. When you're in life-and-death situations, bitterly cold by night and sweating by day in the desert heat, fearing each footstep might land on an improvised explosive device, or round each corner could be a sniper, there's no room for pretence, and our need of one another is sharply focused. Life in the armed forces leads to a strong sense of belonging and depending on one another. Talking to him helped me understand the many homeless ex-servicemen I've met who have ended up on the streets, drinking heavily, often stemming from a strong sense of dislocation once they leave the forces.

The armed forces, for years, have recruited in areas where, through poverty, there are high incidences of family breakdown, so when vulnerable young people from such backgrounds join the army and find a sense of belonging for, perhaps, the first time in their lives, they completely commit themselves to the organisation. For many, the common work and discipline give skills that lead to a much-improved life when they leave the army, but for others, the loss of the strong bonds of community that are rarely replicated outside the army leads to a huge sense of emptiness and purposelessness that, in turn, can lead to a downward spiral of addiction, which often leads to homelessness. Nothing compares to that closeness forged *in extremis* and, when it's taken away, a huge emotional chasm is left.

Historically, the men who never went to war were the miners, who were already doing dangerous and valuable work. Mining communities traditionally had strong ties of social cohesion and a powerful sense of solidarity with the whole trade union movement and organised labour, precisely because of the shared intimacy of dirty and dangerous work. I remember some trade union activists from Tower Hill in Kirkby near Liverpool (where I had my first job as a vicar) being amazed, during a visit to the mining village of Mardy in the Rhonda Valley, by the tightness of that community. They marvelled that people never locked their doors and left the milk money out next to the bottles each week. Sadly, with the closing of the mines in South Wales much of that mutual trust and solidarity has been eroded. Without work, people can so easily lose their dignity, sense of purpose and of belonging, and this can lead to isolation and social exclusion. Writing in *The Guardian*, Aditya Chakrabortty (2017, p.21) highlights how this loss of community has affected the health of a former mining town in the Rhonda Valley:

> A GP in Bargoed estimates that up to one in 10 of her patients have some kind of drug addiction. Up to one in three suffer depression or anxiety. In these parts, a newborn boy can expect to live just over 61 years in good health; in the richest parts of London, it's 75 years.

The loss of much of the UK's manufacturing industry has been mirrored by the breakdown of formerly cohesive communities, particularly in the North of England. The added results of successive government policies of austerity have further eroded any sense of belonging to society, other than as a victim of a cruel and neglectful state. Ken Loach's film *I Daniel Blake* tragically charts the decline of a 59-year-old widowed carpenter who, following a heart attack, is denied benefits despite his cardiologist deeming him unfit to work.

Though having worked with his hands all his adult life, Daniel finds it impossible to navigate the benefits system, as he is not computer literate, and falls into penury. Denied the discipline, social contacts and financial rewards of work, Daniel soon becomes socially excluded and depressed. He is finally granted an appeal, but, at the hearing, the stress of it leads to a further heart attack from which he dies.

In response to austerity and growing poverty in Britain, there has been a growth of food banks (such as the one Daniel Blake visits in the film), school holiday lunch clubs for hungry children, and other charitable responses, which, as well as meeting desperate needs, provide new places outside the workplace for meeting, and they build community for recipients and volunteers alike. Austerity has also begun to stimulate thinking about alternative economic models that are not solely based on the crazy premise of continued growth in a world with finite resources. In her book *Doughnut Economics* Kate Raworth (2017, p.45) makes the argument for a regenerative and distributive economy with a social foundation and an ecological ceiling. She writes, 'What exactly is the Doughnut? Put simply, it's a radically new compass for guiding humanity this century. And it points towards a future that can provide for every person's needs whilst safeguarding the living world on which we all depend.' The journalist George Monbiot (2017a) has suggested that we need what he describes as a 'Politics of Belonging'. Central to his thought is the idea of private sufficiency and public luxury (2017b). He calls for progressive taxation to create a more egalitarian society that consumes much less and calls for massive investment in public services, opportunities for education, leisure participation in sport, the arts, and so on. The dual outcomes of these two policies would be to break down inequalities in our society by raising and lowering incomes but also, by building up public participation, to rebuild a sense of belonging to society.

For Brother Mikela, schooled in the thought of St Benedict and living a life based on the common good of all those living in the monastery, which included a number of asylum seekers, this new way of thinking was nothing new but rather a vindication of the wisdom and sustainability of a way of life which has continued since the seventh century.

After Buddhism spread to China in the third century BCE, monks found they could no longer rely on charitable donations as they had in India, with its tradition of supporting 'sannyasins' and those who had renounced life. Monks in China found they had to work, and work became incorporated into 'zazen', or meditation, and gave purpose as well as providing physical sustenance. The story is told of old Abbott Baizhy who, after his students hid his tools to spare his aged and frail body from work, refused to eat and loudly declared, 'A day without work is a day without food.'

In my life at Pilsdon Community, living amongst many men who had suffered profound social exclusion and were often gruff and uncommunicative, I found that the best way to bond with the men who were most closed off was to work alongside them on a particular practical task. Many of the people who came to us had been defeated by life, and it had been years since some had worked or held down a steady job. In fact, some who'd lived with serious addiction since their youth had never worked. Some of our guests who had a long-term disability or mental illness had effectively been signed off for life and told they would never work again. For others, years of heavy drinking had meant their lives had become so chaotic that no one would employ them for long. Part of the deal when people came to Pilsdon was that no one drank, as we ran the place as a dry house, attendance at meals was compulsory and everyone was expected to work for several hours a day in order to contribute to the running of the farm and household. It didn't matter if it took a person three hours to peel a pan of potatoes most of us would finish in 15 minutes – what was vital was that people were given the opportunity to contribute to the common work of the place.

Pilsdon ran a small farm, had old buildings in constant need of repair and rooms needing constant refurbishment, and with 30-plus people to feed three times a day and a large vegetable garden, had its own little economy and endless opportunities for gainful employment. I started off working in the vegetable garden and slowly built a small team of men and mainly women willing to work with me. The garden was a quarter of an acre square with a rich clay soil enriched with 40 years' worth of animal manure. It was bordered by a south-facing, red-brick wall from a former Victorian greenhouse and the other three sides were sheltered by a hedge. Work in the garden tended to be fairly solitary – endless digging, weeding, and forking out bindweed and couch grass – but we always had a 'gardeners' tea break' when those working would gather for tea and a smoke, and we would sit back and enjoy the beauty and peace of the place.

One man I worked with could identify the song of every bird in the garden. Though prickly and difficult to get on with, he was a brilliant gardener, or 'grower' as he preferred to be called. We first bonded wheeling dozens and dozens of wheelbarrow-loads of well-rotted muck onto one of the fields, dumping it into small rows of mounds and then flinging it round off pitchforks to give an even brown sward. He loved nothing better than to be at one with the soil, and his hands bore the marks of it; where the wet had got into his hands and cracked the skin the soil had followed and left him with a kind of earthy stigmata. These really were marks of love, for he told me that it was nature that had saved his life – or rather prevented him from taking it. Abuse in his early life had left him almost permanently angry and unable to fully trust anyone; for him, only nature was constant and consistent, and being outdoors was what brought him a sense of peace. As I worked with him over the years, a kind of trust grew between us through our common love of the earth and trust in the integrity of Creation.

However, most of the men at Pilsdon didn't want to work on the land, for they saw gardening as somehow feminine, which perhaps it is. Francis of Assisi, in his thirteenth-century 'Canticle of the Creatures', sings of Mother Earth, and prior to that and amongst Pagans today, there's a long tradition of earth deities being female. As many of the men who pitched up at Pilsdon were often rather 'unreconstructed' types, I began to realise that to get alongside them, I'd have to engage in something more outwardly macho such as construction work. The community had a generous maintenance budget, as much to create meaningful work for people as to repair the fabric of the place, for we realised that for the community to function well, people's hands needed to be busy, minds focused and kept in the moment.

The first bit of building work I did at Pilsdon was the digging and construction of a duck pond. I worked with Richard, a big, swarthy, red-faced man, who'd been in the building trade for a number of years, and he moved around confidently and, happy in his work, sang doleful Country and Western songs. I was new and terribly keen, like a young Labrador puppy, ready at his beck and call. The first thing he taught me, and something I've never forgotten, was how to load a shovel not so much using your back but scraping the shovel along the ground and picking up sand and gravel by pushing your knee behind the shaft of the shovel. 'That'll save your back in the future,' he told me and, thousands of shovels later, I've never forgotten that lesson and passed it on to numerous others. As we dug out the hole for what was growing into something more like a small swimming pool, and I barrowed away the spoil, he began to tell me about his life.

He'd been in the army for many years and spent nearly as long in prison: as he put it, 'I've served over 25 years in Her Majesty's institutions.' He'd gone to prison on a charge of manslaughter for killing a man in a fight. He'd been drunk at the time, and told me how drink had robbed him of his freedom but, more importantly, had been the major factor in the destruction of his marriage. Working each day with him, beyond the songs and the banter, I sensed a hidden anger and, as I looked at his powerful hands gripping the shovel, I decided not to upset him.

As the days passed, the pond began to take shape and as it grew, so Richard seemed to grow in confidence and feel more part of the place, and our relationship also developed. One conversation I remember having with him was about the different roles and different power people exercised in the community. He got really angry one day when the leader of the community told him he couldn't get a lift into town the day he wanted and he'd have to wait and go on the community shopping trip that went every Wednesday. He was so mad that he walked the seven miles into town and back the next day. His face was purple-red when he returned, mirroring his anger, for he felt there was one rule for guests like him and another for the core community like me who had the responsibility for running the place.

The difference had already made me feel uncomfortable as I, at times, had access to a car, better accommodation, a separate day off and outwardly more freedom than our guests. I felt I knew him well enough to have it out with him and I stood up to him, absorbing some of his anger, and then explained my thinking on the different positions we were in. First of all, I told him there was no difference between us as men. I told him I believed we were all made in God's image and equal as such. Where there was difference, it was in our different roles in the community. As a community member, I was here for the long haul and had responsibilities around organising work, keeping the prayer life of the community going, keeping alive its Christian vision and holding the boundaries around acceptable behaviour, in particular enforcing, if necessary, our total ban on alcohol and drugs. These responsibilities meant I had a different role in the community, not that I thought I was any better than him or wished to wield power or authority over him. I also wasn't going to apologise for living in better accommodation than him, as I had a wife and three children to support. He took my explanation graciously, and I told him our conversation had helped me begin to work out how I was to live in the community.

Without our common experience of working together, I don't think we'd have been able to have such an honest exchange. The great gift, for me, of manual work was that, in spite of different roles and expectations in the community, there was always the possibility to show the intrinsic equality of our life together by getting in a ditch and digging, shovelling cement or peeling a huge bowl of potatoes together with our guests.

After a couple of weeks the pond was ready to fill, which took several hours, and then the ducks were released onto it and happily quacked away. A few weeks later, Richard was gone but the pond remained as a reminder of the practical skills he'd taught me, the wisdom he'd evoked from me and the friendship we'd formed.

Over the years, every now and then he'd ring me, often drunk, but never failing to ask how the duck pond was.

WORK BUILDS FRIENDSHIP

My work with Richard set a pattern and style of how I knew I wanted to work alongside people. I'd discovered that manual work could be a great equaliser and offered a way of coming to know people in a natural, non-threatening and mutual kind of way. So much of people's working lives in the West is now sedentary, perhaps sitting at a computer and next to a phone, or in a car or van and usually rushing to meet a deadline. Much of it is quite solitary, and many now do 'remote' working from home. Even the farmers around us at Pilsdon usually spent most of their day alone, driving huge tractors with air-conditioned cabs and pulling ever more sophisticated farm machinery. I often wondered what they thought, looking down from their massive tractors and watching four or five people take a week to spread muck over a field with wheelbarrows and forks – a job they would have done in a couple of hours with their expensive kit. I knew though which method I preferred, and it was the old one, which gave time to look at the venerable old oaks that lined the fields and hear the rooks in their newly built February nests and, most precious of all, gave me time to spend with others and, through sharing a common task, build up our life together.

Percy Smith, who founded Pilsdon in 1958, was very aware of the importance of manual work in building up common life and he saw it also as a way of giving praise to God. In one of his early 'Letters from a Community', he quotes Gerard Manley Hopkins: 'To lift up the hands in prayer gives God Glory, but a man with a dung fork in his hand or a woman with a slop pail give him glory too. God is so great that all things give him glory if you mean that they should' (Smith 1962, p.12).

One of the highlights for me of life at Pilsdon, was our twice-yearly emptying of the cow's winter quarters. Over the winter, twice a day we'd shake fresh straw onto the old straw and dung to provide soft and warm bedding for our Jersey milk cows in the small barn that sheltered them. After a few months, their floor would gradually rise to the extent that they would start banging their heads on the low ceiling, which meant it was time to dig out several tonnes of impacted dung. We had no tractor so relied on forks and wheelbarrows and bodies to push them. Three of us would start digging and another 15 would offer up their empty barrows to be filled. These would then be pushed several hundred yards to where a new muck heap would be constructed by a couple of others, organising scaffolding planks as running boards. One year, the heap got so big we misnamed it after the highest point on the Dorset coast, 'Golden Crap'. The work, of course, was pure gold as it brought the whole community out; even those who couldn't push a barrow would help with lunch or provide tea on the hour, every hour. It was dirty, back-breaking work, but always fun and, because everyone joined in, it engendered a sense of community. When you're covered in shit, the smell of it seeping out of your pores, it's a great leveller and reminder of our common humanity.

The Austin Zen Centre in Texas talks about work as both building community and developing the individual: 'Work brings us together as a community. When there's real physical work we struggle and sweat together and create a place together and that place inspires our practice on a daily basis, because we know we have worked to make it' (Austin Zen Centre 2019).

WORK BUILDS TRUST

Physical work reminds us that we belong together, makes us aware of our human frailty and makes concrete our dependence on one another. All the years I was at Pilsdon, there was a guest who'd been there for many years and encapsulated what it meant to live well in community. John said little, but his gentle presence was always a great reassurance. He was always up first, milked the cows and would make breakfast for the whole community. He did a lot of the hidden work – he disposed of the rubbish, burnt brash, rodded blocked sewers and did loads of washing up. He was enormously strong and whenever a delivery arrived, he was always there to help unload. Whenever you were struggling with digging a ditch or moving logs and others had left, he would mysteriously appear and give fresh impetus to the job. Likewise, he would also just disappear if you were doing a more interesting job and others arrived to share in the enjoyment of it. One winter's day, we were barrowing well-rotted dung from the muck heap along perilously slippery scaffolding boards to the vegetable garden, when John slipped and fell off the board horizontally into a pool of slurry next to it. He stood up covered from head to toe, calmly wiped his glasses and carried on as if nothing had happened. Stoic.

I came to understand that to live well in community I had to let John be my mentor. He was a man of few words and would never tell me how to be in community, but I knew if I watched and imitated him I'd learn more about community than in all the endless books written about it. Still today, when getting frustrated with someone, or feeling worn out by a task, I ask myself, 'What would John do?' His gentle presence and humility continue to teach me about how to be with others. Learning to be attentive to others, to be comfortable in silence, companionable working and the gift of another pair of hands are all vital to how we learn to belong together.

In contrast to the corruption that too often seems to emanate from those at the top end of industry, commerce and banking, there's an honesty and dignity that come from hard physical labour. When you're working with someone on a roof, you need to be able to trust them completely. I was taught roofing by 'Scouse' Pete, one of the most dishonest people I've ever met. He came to Pilsdon following a two-year sentence for multiple offences as a confidence trickster. He'd particularly targeted vulnerable older people, getting money up front for roofing materials to repair non-existent damage he had spotted whilst walking past. He conned people to fuel a gambling addiction, and he would try anything to get money to gamble. He was a fanatical Liverpool supporter and he bet compulsively on football matches. Once he claimed our pigs had eaten his Levi jeans from the washing line and demanded we reimburse him their cost.

I congratulated him on the originality of his story and told him it made a change from hearing the story of needing the train fare to visit a dying grandma in Glasgow. We pretty much grounded him at the community to try and prevent his betting (this was in the days before the prevalence of online betting), but he still managed to gamble by proxy, convincing others to gamble on his behalf.

He was a skilled roofer, who'd done an apprenticeship with a renowned roof tile specialist, and working on the roof with him, I saw a different side to him. Setting up scaffolding, stripping bare a roof and then re-laying the slates with him, I realised what a skilled worker he was and, lost in the job, he somehow became honest, as he shared his story with me and I saw the real person he was before his addiction took over. I joked with him that I was proud to be taught roofing by a con man, and for a couple of weeks we happily lost ourselves in the job of getting the barn roof on before the rains came. Sadly he continued to gamble and we had to ask him to leave, but I know if I see him again, I'll be pleased to see him as a fellow roofer rather than the person we excluded from the community. I'd never have got to know the real Pete if we'd been sat all day in an office together and we hadn't made use of his skills; by becoming his student and working with him, I learnt much and I hope he somehow imbibed something of the spirit of generosity and acceptance that flowed through the community and our challenge to him to confront his addictive and destructive behaviour.

MANUAL WORK BUILDS SOLIDARITY WITH EACH OTHER

Manual labour is something that encourages people to be straightforward and open with one another and breaks down inbuilt notions of hierarchy where some, through their roles, class or ethnic background, are better than others. Sadly, the Church of England, on whose fringes I've operated for the past 30 years, is full of hierarchy and pomposity. It's very good at proclaiming the faith, getting people to profess what they believe and writing reports about social inequality but not always good at getting alongside people in their daily struggles. In contrast to the top-down Roman Catholic Church of its day, the worker-priest movement in post-Second-World-War France sought a different model of being alongside those excluded from established religion. The movement had grown out of the experience of a number of Roman Catholic priests in German-occupied France who had been deported to Germany as prisoners of war. They had hidden their priestly status and had endured the hardships of others in the prison camps. One of these 'hidden priests' was Henri Perrin, who on his return to France published his experiences in *Priest and Worker: The Autobiography of Henri Perrin* (1965). This book, along with the experiences of older priests who'd found real engagement with working-class soldiers in the trenches of the First World War, led to the founding of the worker-priest movement. Priests would work on the factory shop floor, sharing simple manual labour and receiving the same low wages and poor working conditions of their fellow workers. By 1951, there were 87 worker-priests in Paris alone, but because of their involvement in labour protests and strikes, the movement was supressed by the French bishops due to pressure from factory owners.

In England, inspired by their French colleagues, two Anglican ministers, Michael Gedge and John Strong, went to work in the East Kent coalfield and worked underground on the conveyor belt at Eythorne Colliery. They worked and lived along their fellow miners in a ministry of radical accompaniment. John Mantle, in his book *Britain's First Worker-Priests* (2000), stresses the different approach between these two worker-priests and the establishment-supported Sheffield Industrial Mission:

> While Ted Whickham's men donned boiler suits and walked into the workplace to meet men and then left the works, Gedge and Strong, stripped to the waist and sometimes working alone in stifling darkness for the sake of the safety of the other men underground, cleaned the conveyor belts that brought the coal to the surface. (p.125)

My life at Pilsdon shared something of this mutual solidarity with others, and I found that working alongside men and women who had been marginalised by the rest of society needed a certain patience, humility and sensitivity. I discovered that if you found the right job for somebody, they could thrive and grow in confidence. Sometimes I was the instructor, perhaps showing someone how to lay a course of bricks, but more often than not I was the apprentice, learning new decorating skills or how to plaster a wall. I loved this reversal of skills where I, the leader of the community, became the labourer for the skilled worker who might have been homeless a couple of weeks before. It bred mutual trust and respect between us.

Learning to mentor and support others is a skill that is too often undervalued in the world of work, where production and outcomes become the overriding priority. Where personal achievement and individual success are the main goals, stress and the lack of time to build meaningful relationships are inevitable results. Friends working in education and the National Health Service tell me that the constant pressures of bureaucratic accountability to managers and inspectors mean that the really meaningful work of teaching children and spending time with patients becomes limited to the bare minimum. The pursuit of efficiency has led to an undervaluing of relationships and a lack of time to pass on your skills to others. Jenny, who now lives at Hilfield Friary, told me of how she had always dreamed of nursing and had gone back into education as a mature student in order to qualify for nurse training. She worked for 15 years in the health service but left disillusioned, as the more qualified and experienced she became, the less time she had with patients. She said, 'I left because I was no longer able to spend time with patients, I was no longer nursing patients but managing a busy ward. There was never any slack, never any time just to be with the patients. That's not what I went into nursing to do.'

Having the time to be with people and to be literally hands-on with them as a nurse needs to be rediscovered if we are to have a more holistic health service.

WORK CAN BE HEALING

A young man called Nick came to stay with us at Hilfield Friary. He'd lost his job, his relationship had broken down, leaving him homeless and sleeping in his car, and he'd become severely depressed. He arrived thin and pasty-looking, was very withdrawn. Every morning at 10 a.m., I went to knock on his bedroom door, checking he was still with us, as I feared that such was his despair, he might take his own life. What we were able to offer him at the friary were the conditions for him to get well. A peaceful place, people around him, regular meals and, crucially, work to join in with. Slowly, he began to engage with us, and I knew he had painting and decorating skills, so I asked him if he'd help me repoint a wall. We set up the scaffolding and began the painstaking task of knocking out the old mortar between the flint and local stone and filling it with a creamy-textured mix of lime mortar. The job went on for a couple of weeks and slowly his motivation improved and he began to get himself up. Soon, the wall was pointed to a much higher standard than I could ever have managed and when we had finished and put the scaffolding away, I said to him, 'There's one more thing we need to do.'

'What's that?' he asked.

'The most important thing,' I replied. 'Stand back and admire our work.'

There's such a joy in completing a task well; it's good sometimes just to look and look again at our work. I said to him, 'I think that's what they call in Dorset a "proper Job".'

We worked on a whole variety of construction jobs and, increasingly, he became my tutor and was almost instantly better at any new skill I was able to teach him. He also became a great accompanier to others suffering with depression, patiently listening to their woes and occasionally commenting helpfully but always without judgement. I particularly enjoyed the way he'd tactfully persuade me to change my method of work: 'Jonathan, have you ever thought of doing it this way?', he'd gently suggest. He received good support from the community mental health team and did some mindfulness sessions, and later asked me, 'You know when you're really lost in a job, fully concentrating on it, such as painting a windowsill, isn't that a kind of mindfulness?'

I'm sure that it is. My experience of doing a repetitive job, such as nailing hundreds of tiles on a roof, is that it's a way of losing yourself in the present moment, and it can feel wonderfully liberating. If I compare the difference in my mood after spending an afternoon tiling a roof to after spending a couple of hours in a meeting, I know which one leaves me feeling most at peace with myself and others. Nick left us almost a year to the day he had arrived but as a person full of renewed confidence, looking forward to a future full of promise, though also living one day at a time.

Work with the hands can be so healing, as it can return confidence and dignity and restore a sense of connection with the natural rhythms of life. To dig the ground, to pick up a hammer, to thread a needle, to knead a lump of dough, even for the first time, feels instinctively right and a natural occupation for our hands. Today so many hands are idle, or just their tips are touching keyboards or remote controls, or tapping touch screens, and work has become physically passive, sedentary and often solitary. This has led to a rise in obesity and deteriorating mental health, lack of exercise leading to weight gain and lone working leading to a sense of isolation, which, coupled with the constant demands to work longer and more competitively, inevitably leads to growing levels of anxiety. People are now being encouraged to adopt the practice of 'remote working', using their homes as their office. This undoubtedly has its benefits in cutting down traffic congestion and saving people travel time, but can also blur the boundaries between work and time off and inevitably, as the name suggests, lead to a sense of isolation. The growing popularity of 'life coaches' can be seen as a desire for people to lead a more balanced and active life, and how we need others to encourage and assist us in this process.

Ted, who farmed land next to Pilsdon, was a wonderful life coach. He'd lived in the same 500-year-old thatched farmhouse for 70 years, he always wore the same ancient military beret and tattered trousers, held up with bailer twine, and drove an aged Ford tractor, which he spent several minutes coaxing into life each morning.

I first got to know him and our neighbouring farmers when we worked together renewing a water pipe that fed several of the farms from a spring on the hillside. Our friendship began through digging together and continued to grow and deepen as we shared in several practical projects. It was the tree work I did with him and others that really bound us together. He had about 30 acres of land, smallish fields bounded by hedges containing dozens of second-generation ash poles rising to some 40 feet high in places, and he'd decided it was time to fell them and lay his hedges. I'd find myself at the foot of one of the ash trees with the chainsaw running, with a cotton strap attached at one end to the top of the tree I'd just climbed, and Ted would be at the other end tying the strap to his tractor, shouting incomprehensible instructions in his broad Dorset dialect. The tree always seemed to be leaning over a fence, so the strap was necessary to try to pull it back to prevent it falling and damaging the fence, which meant felling it was a bit unpredictable. Every now and then, the tree would fall in an unexpected direction and I'd jump out of the way, and Ted would then come over and, grinning, say, 'That wore a bit close weren't it?'

I loved working with Ted because he was such a gentle, deeply contented man, utterly part of the land on which he lived, and always with a twinkle in his eye and a kindly word. When one of the guests at Pilsdon was particularly stressed or out of sorts, I'd often take them over to see Ted and we'd do some logging together, and the combination of his kindly presence, his sense of purpose and a few hours of heavy work seemed profoundly healing for whoever came. He'd hardly say anything to them, but his gentle presence, rooted firmly in the soil, time and again transformed people's mood. He was a great accompanier.

There's something about being physically present to each other that makes all the difference: a handwritten letter, email, telephone call, Skype or even 'face time' are not the same as an embodied encounter. Trying to learn how to do a job by watching someone on YouTube, though always helpful, is never the same as having the person present, communicating much more than the words they use.

Sometimes, just turning up for someone is the most important thing we can do. It doesn't matter what we say, just being there for someone can be hugely reassuring and give hope in the direst of circumstances. Accompaniment isn't just about accompanying the mind or the soul, but being with the whole person. Picking up a large tree trunk on Ted's farm and loading it onto the back of his trailer, smelling the sweat of the person next to you, hearing them grunt, and turning and smiling at them as you let go of its weight together is the kind of embodied encounter that connects us in the simplest and most natural of ways. Shared work that gives purpose is always restorative.

There's a scheme run by the courts that we're part of at Hilfield, called 'Community Payback', which supervises people who've been given non-custodial sentences. Instead of doing time in prison, offenders are instructed to do a set number of hours of community work. It's a way to give people a second chance, and also to make amends for the offences they've committed by putting something back into the community. We take people on a Saturday, which has the advantage to the community that we often get some very skilled workers who would be working during weekdays. We never ask what their offences are, but rather what their skills are, and try and make use of them. So if we have a carpenter, we'll have her repairing a window, or a cook, we'll encourage him to work in the kitchen. If people are unskilled, and there are some young people who come who have never worked, we will try and find a project that they can work with us on. I'm told that too much of the time other placements are dull and repetitive, doing things such as picking up litter from road verges all day. Nearly everybody who comes to us finishes their hours, and the community benefits from a lot of skilled and unskilled labour. The key to the scheme working well is the quality of the supervisors, and we're lucky that we have George and Graham, two really good supervisors.

WORK HELPS US BELONG

There's a real need in our society to fill in the gaps for those people and communities who seem forgotten and become isolated, feel excluded and because of a loss of traditional forms of manual work feel a sense of emptiness and dislocation, and often succumb to addiction and anti-social behaviour. My work with Gypsies and Travellers, who many regard as the most hated and socially excluded group in the UK, has confirmed to me that the loss of the opportunity to both travel and work with their hands has led to very high incidences of poor mental health, addiction and suicide. Father John Chadwick, who works with Irish Travellers, says that suicide amongst young men from this community is at epidemic proportions. One of the reasons for this is a sense of purposelessness, as people from this traditionally hardworking community find the traditional manual labour they used to do is no longer there or has been taken up by others. Since their arrival in this country in 1514, Romany Gypsies have faced constant persecution by the state and individuals, but managed to survive by their resourcefulness and ability to live off the land, and became vital seasonal workers in the agricultural economy.

The older Gypsies I meet talk of a hard but much-loved life revolving around the seasons, moving from picking elderflowers in the spring to cropping peas and beans, then helping with the hay harvest, fruit picking, potato lifting and cutting sugar beet in the winter. There are stories of people cutting off fingers in the winter and not noticing at first because their hands were so numb with the cold. They lived outdoors, working in the fields by day and gathering round the fire by night for food and conversation. In Dorset, there is much hostility to Gypsies amongst the younger farmers, but talk to any farmer over 70 and they'll often have positive stories about Gypsies who parked up on their land every year and were a vital and trusted part of their seasonal workforce.

Sadly, most of the old stopping places, or 'atchin tans', have been lost to post-war house building, industrial estates and country parks. This, combined with legislation such as the 1968 Caravans

Act and the Criminal Justice Bill of 1994, has made it almost impossible for nomadic people to travel, and many have been forced into what they describe as 'the darkness' of brick houses. At the same time, the mechanisation of agriculture, the regulation of scrap metal dealing, and the change in the law that has virtually criminalised cold-calling to sell flowers, baskets and clothes pegs door to door has led to a loss of income but also of traditional skills in the community. Traditionally, levels of literacy have been low in the Gypsy community because of the difficulty of getting schooling whilst on the move, and children, so often bullied at school, were reluctant to go. This was never a problem when lots of unskilled work was available, but now to get a job nearly everybody requires the ability to read and write. Something as basic as taking the 'theory' part of the driving test requires the ability to read. With the loss of manual forms of work, as well as the obvious economic disadvantage, has come a feeling of uselessness and the loss of their sense of identity. Damian Le Bas (2018, p.65), Romany Gypsy and writer, describes how the industrialisation of agriculture has led to a loss not just of work, but also identity: 'It was surprising to think that the mechanisation of agriculture had begun so far back in the past. To Travellers it was the still recent scapegoat for everything: the amoral and inevitable creeping phenomenon that had robbed us of our place.'

In Dorset, we have a group called 'Kushti Bok', meaning 'good luck' in Romany, which is made up of local Gypsies, Irish Travellers and New Travellers. We seek to be a positive voice for Travellers and challenge discrimination in the media, and have teamed up with a local agricultural college to encourage Travellers to learn crafts such as blacksmithing, basket making, work with horses and floristry in order to revive these skills in the community. Core to the wellbeing and pride of the Gypsy and Traveller community, I believe, is a need to recover the lost art of manual work, and that, I think, is true for all of us. The greater our disconnection from the land and physical dexterity, the more we endanger our sense of wellbeing.

I learnt the art of peg making from Caleb, who was born in a horse-drawn, bow top wagon, in which he travelled with his parents all across southern England. I met him on my first day of work as chaplain to Gypsies and Travellers at a Gypsy heritage day in Dorchester. He was sitting under a tree on a canvas sheet next to a pile of wood shavings, knocking out dozens of clothes pegs. I sat down next to him and asked if I could have a go, and for the next hour he taught me with patience and good humour: first, how to shave a two-foot length of hazel, then how to chop it into four peg lengths, then to pin a thin collar of tin around the top, then the splitting of the peg from the base upwards and a deft 180-degree turn of the blade to clean out the inside of the peg, and finally two swift cuts to shape the end of the peg. He could make two dozen pegs in the twenty minutes it took me to make mine. I made two more before the hour was up and only then introduced myself as the new chaplain, and thanked him for my first lesson in Gypsy culture. It felt like a good way to start my work with Travellers, sitting on the ground alongside Caleb, working with my fingers to begin my education in Gypsy heritage. Four years on, I still carry the peg in my jacket pocket, and slowly the wood is being worn smooth as I sometimes stroke it inadvertently. It sometimes comes in handy too as a prompt when talking to an older Gypsy, or as a visual aid when I give talks about Gypsy and Traveller culture.

To such events I'll often take a Gypsy calling basket that I've made, and tell how men and women would have made them from willow and hazel from the hedgerow, and the women and children would have filled them with spring flowers to sell in the street or door to door. I always feel better for making a basket, and best of all when I've sat with someone and taught them how to make one. Basket making is one of the oldest crafts, long predating pottery, and every part of the world you go to has its own style and local materials suitable for weaving into baskets. I've sat with weavers in the Gambia, Uganda and the Pacific Islands and learnt their craft. Making things together, sat on the ground in the shade of a tree, is such a lovely way to build common ground with another.

WORK IS CREATIVE

The term 'basket case' came from the prevalence of basket making in psychiatric hospitals, where its calming properties have been long recognised. Sitting on the floor with your back propped against a wall weaving repetitively in and out and slowly turning the basket in a circular motion, which I tell people reminds me that the earth we live on is slowly turning, is a well-proven way of staying in the moment and letting go of troubling thoughts. The willow I use will have been soaked for a few hours and left to mellow overnight so it's soft to the touch and pliable. Once the base has been woven, the sides are staked up and then the willow is woven in and out horizontally with slightly thinner withies, gently forced down to fill any gaps. Quickly the basket takes shape as the weavers build up the sides and, as the hands are kept busy and the eyes concentrate on the work in hand, so the mind gives way a little and less-guarded conversations are free to develop. It's amazing how many meaningful conversations I've had whilst sitting with my student building the sides of our baskets up. Just as precious too are the almost silent hours I've sat with another as we've both lost ourselves in the process of making our baskets. Whether the process is silent or avuncular, finishing off the basket always seems to bring a sense of joy and wonder. I always encourage people to put their new basket somewhere they can see it for the first 24 hours of having it, and keep admiring it every now and then, watching how the light plays on it, noticing the shadows between alternate weaves and just delighting in it. It's much cheaper to buy a plastic wastepaper bin, but you can't put a value on something made with your own hands and with another.

Sam Hale, who works as a community arts worker across the West Midlands with a lot with marginalised women, maintains that busy hands lead to much sharing. When fingers are occupied and concentrating on sewing a bit of material or adding pieces to a mosaic, somehow the mind's defences are lowered and a deep level of disclosure can happen. If people are shy or lacking in confidence, she says, working with your hands allows you to avoid eye contact, yet still talk. Also, for someone very withdrawn working on a practical project allows them to be part of the group without the need to speak. By sharing practical work people can rediscover a sense of belonging, and isolation can be overcome by talking together or just being able to sit quietly in the group, saying nothing but sharing a communal task. The five years I worked on the Beechdale council estate we employed Sam and her husband Karl in a number of capacities, such as organising an arts week, carnival procession, and costumes for a community play. We employed them as skilled artists in their own right, but their real value to the community was their intuitive and highly skilled way of working alongside people. Sam would say that a mixture of practical tasks with a creative end are sure and tested ways of building trust and openness between people. In her work, Sam maintains that the process is always more important than the final product, and that the work with people is of greater value than the final exhibition. As she writes, 'Every work of art has its lover and critic, and community art is no exception. There is always a trade off when you are working on group projects, as you balance the quality of the process and the quality of the product' (Webster 1997, p.49).

The journey with is more important than the final destination, but of course if you engage well and authentically with people in the lead-up to an event, the results are also likely to have a quality and artistic integrity.

Manual work can be restorative for individuals, and accompanying others in this way doubly so, but I want to turn now to the question as to whether accompaniment has the power not just to break down differences between individuals, but also to radically challenge the polarisation of whole groups of people.

5

CROSSING THE DIVIDE

It was nearly 7 p.m. and the large community hall was filling up. As we thought, there was going to be a massive response to the public meeting that had been called. The local community in the Coburg Road area of Dorchester was here to vent its anger against the Pilsdon Community, who were planning to open a house in this leafy and respectable part of town. Everyone who came through the door was asked to write down their name and address, and issued with a name badge. Everyone was offered tea, but our hospitality was met with stony-faced refusal. The fear and anger in the room was palpable; no one would look us in the eye and all went straight to their seats. There was a buzz in the room but it wasn't that feeling of anticipation before the show begins, but rather a toxic mix of prejudice, anger and deep uncertainty.

Pilsdon Community was planning to open a 'move-on' house in Dorchester, in order to provide somewhere safe and supportive for people to be when they leave the community, to allow people to continue their recovery when they no longer have the protection of the community, rather than lapse back into depression or the cycle of addiction. We had identified a former nursing home with room for 12 people, which seemed ideal, and the town of Dorchester provided opportunities for training, work and volunteering. We already had the requisite planning permission to open the house, but we decided to introduce Pilsdon to those living nearby to calm any of their potential fears. We'd envisaged a small meeting with our immediate neighbours and some representatives of the local community. One of the neighbours, though, sent out an inflammatory letter to over 200 houses in the streets around the house, letting people know that the house would be full of drug addicts, alcoholics and former prisoners and asking the loaded question, 'Will our children be safe?' Two days before the meeting, similar headlines were on the front page of the *Dorset Echo*, and the day it was due to take place, Radio Wessex broadcast the upcoming meeting on its hourly news bulletin.

We were expecting trouble but had planned for it. The reason each individual was given a name badge was to identify them, which we felt would make them more accountable and not just part of a mob. We had a panel of two smartly dressed clergymen, a former politician, and our chair of trustees, Dr James Cairns OBE, in a linen suit. James chaired the meeting with great gravitas and authority and named each member of the public as he invited them to speak. The meeting began well with an open and transparent explanation of Pilsdon's history, the discipline of our common life, with emphasis on our zero tolerance for any kind of anti-social behaviour, our management of risk, and our vetting procedures for people applying to join the community.

Things went well until a local parent got up to speak, who passionately harangued the assembly for not supporting us, and at that point, just as we had feared, the meeting exploded into life. False accusations of underhand dealing in the planning process were thrown at us, fears about paedophiles being housed with us, and the likelihood of theft and criminal damage were bellowed at us. Somehow our chair kept calm and wisely invited the community policeman to speak. He stood up and, for a moment, the meeting calmed. He told the meeting that 200 yards from the hall was a private house where people dealt heroin and crack cocaine, but the police could do little about closing it down as it was a private dwelling. He then went on to reiterate Pilsdon's checks and balances around governance, and the discipline and boundaries outlined in our common life. He ended by saying, 'I know which house I'd rather live next door to.'

At that moment, the meeting began to shift. Local friends we'd planted in the meeting began to sing the praises of the community and before the meeting ended, we'd set up a visit to Pilsdon for our new neighbours and people were asking what they might do to help the new household. It was a remarkable transformation where, through real open engagement, fear and hostility had given way to dialogue and the possibility of friendship.

OTHERING

In our divided and often polarised world, there's a great need for people who are prepared to cross the artificial boundaries we create between peoples: those who, like that policeman, are prepared to stand up to the vilification of communities, examine the facts and hear people's stories, and expose that shallow but weighty prejudice that diminishes us all. It's so much easier to listen to our own fears and anxieties and build a collective fear of the 'other' rather than have the courage to cross the divide and make the time to sit down with the stranger and discover that they aren't that strange or different to us after all.

Social media, whilst being a great vehicle to bring communities together, too often is used as a tool to spread hatred and sectarianism and emphasise division. Its remote nature makes it ideal for this, as you never need to look the person whom you abuse in the eye and don't need to respond to their anger, fear and anguish, yet you can still feel part of the mob who urge each other on with viler and viler tweets. It's a little like warfare conducted by drone; at little risk to yourself you can command a strike without seeing the consequences of your actions. In her book *Why I'm No Longer Talking to White People about Race*, Reni Eddo-Lodge (2017, p.118) charts the history and extent of othering in relation to black people in the UK: 'The projection of an ever-encroaching black doomsday is what I call "fear of a black planet". It's a fear that the alienated "other" will take over. Enoch Powell's fears of a flipped script have lived on in modern-day political rhetoric on immigration.'

Rarely in all the recent debates in this country on immigration do we ever think about what has forced people to leave home and family and take huge risks to get here. It's far easier to see refugees as a threat rather than people having a story and a history, part of which is heavily influenced by British colonialism and foreign policy.

In her lecture 'Let them drown: The violence of othering in a warming world', Naomi Klein (2016, p.2) quotes Palestinian academic Edward Said, whom she describes as a giant in the study of 'othering'. He describes 'othering' in his book *Orientalism* as 'disregarding, essentialising, denuding the humanity of another culture, people or geographical region'. She goes on to explain how governments and corporations have got away with extracting dirty, environmentally damaging fossil fuels by belittling the people in the regions of extractions. Mountaintops are blown off in the Appalachian hills to cheaply extract coal on the premise that the locals are only 'hillbillies', who don't really care about their hills. Conflict in the Middle East, she argues, has been legitimised by the practice of othering. She describes 'the project of Orientalism, of "othering" Arab and Muslim people', who she says have been described as 'other, exotic, primitive, bloodthirsty'. Othering makes it far easier to wage wars and stage coups in order to keep cheap oil flowing to the West. The overthrow of the democratically elected government of Muhammed Mossadegh in Iran in 1953 through British and US collaboration when he prepared to nationalise the Anglo–Persian Oil Company (later to become BP) was such an example, as was the invasion of Iraq some 50 years later.

The burning of fossil fuels, and our foolish short-sighted dependence on them, she argues, has only been made possible by our separating ourselves from the suffering of the native peoples, such as those in the Niger Delta, and the corresponding suffering and extinction of many forms of life, destroyed by global warming. She calls for a joined-up, more holistic approach, considering that we are all adversely affected by the warming of our planet and, as such, inextricably linked together. She contrasts the 'let them drown' rhetoric of parts of the Australian government with the words of Liam Cox, who was concerned that parts of the media, such as the

Daily Mail, were using the 2015 floods in England to increase anti-foreigner sentiments: 'Why should we be giving foreign aid when we can't afford our own flood defences?' He writes from Hebden Bridge, an area badly affected by flooding:

> All you morons vomiting your xenophobia...about how money should only be spent 'on our own' need to look at yourselves closely in the mirror. I request you ask yourself a very important question... Am I a decent and honourable human being? Because home isn't just the UK, home is everywhere on the planet. (Klein, 2016)

In the same way, for the people at the public meeting in Dorchester, their willingness to condemn the people from Pilsdon, who they thought weren't like them, could only be maintained as long as they were seen as other. Once that narrative was challenged and, crucially, later on, as opponents of the house met residents at Pilsdon, their fears fell away. That embodied encounter with real people was what won our neighbours over and dismantled their previous notions of otherness.

SCAPEGOATING

How we encourage individuals, groups, communities and national governments to challenge this practice of othering is an urgent question for our time, as it has been throughout history. The apparent human need to define ourselves against the 'other', then vilify and scapegoat them has been around for millennia. The Jewish people realised this human predilection to look for someone to blame and created a ritual to allow people to dump all their fear, frustration and anxiety once a year onto a goat set aside for the purpose. On the Day of Atonement, the priest would lay his hands on the goat and pass on the sins of all the people onto the animal; the goat would then be led into the wilderness and set free:

> Then Aaron shall lay both his hands on the head of the live goat, and confess over it all the iniquities of the people of Israel, and all their transgressions, all their sins, putting them on the head of the goat, and sending it away into the wilderness by means of someone designated for the task. The goat shall bear on itself all their iniquities to a barren region; and the goat shall be set free in the wilderness. (Leviticus 16:21–22)

Here we see, enshrined in ritual, an understanding of the human desire to blame someone else for all our ills, insecurities and fears, and a ritual enactment that attempts to work it out without recourse to violence. Notice that the goat is not slaughtered but rather released into the wilderness. French philosopher, social anthropologist and literary critic Rene Girard has written extensively on the recurrence of the theme of the scapegoat in primitive and modern societies. Describing scapegoating he writes, 'By the Scapegoat effect I mean that strange process by which two or more people are reconciled at the expense of a third party, who appears guilty or responsible for whatever ails, disturbs or frightens the scapegoaters' (Williams 1996, p.12). He goes on to talk of corporate prejudice: 'Scapegoat effects are not just limited to mobs but are most conspicuously effective in the case of mobs. The destruction of a victim can make a mob more furious, but it can also bring a sense of tranquillity' (Williams 1996, p.12).

On 20 August 2017, a mob of some 200 people assembled to protest at an unauthorised Traveller encampment in Weston-super-Mare, where some 20 homeless Irish Travellers parked on Baytree playing fields. The police eventually dispersed the angry locals and escorted the Travellers out of the town. What worried me about this scenario was the possibility of vigilante violence, and it will be extremely disturbing for all groups of nomadic people if it becomes a pattern across the country. Travellers I know, who are still on the road, tell me of abuse and threats on a daily basis from angry locals, but this mass demonstration in Weston marked a worrying escalation and organisation of anger, fear and prejudice. *The Sun* headline was aimed at egging others on: '"OUT! OUT! OUT!" Dramatic moment hundreds of angry locals including children confronted Travellers who had moved into Weston-super-Mare park' (Devlin 2017). *The Sun*'s Facebook page was full of derogatory comments:

> here we go again, the British public doing the cops job...useless police scared of upsetting the 'pykies', no wonder they do what they want, when they want, leaving tonnes of crap that costs us 10s of thousands every time to clear it up. (Geff Allan)

> Shoot the Bastards and get rid of the leftie yogurt knitters.

> Travellers are nothing more than VERMIN, what do we do with vermin? call in pest control and eradicate the problem by whatever means. (Peter Pan)

The word 'vermin' was a favoured Nazi term used to dehumanise the Jews. The Nazis described Gypsies as 'Zigeuner' (untouchable). In Rwanda the word 'cockroaches' was used to describe the Tutsis. The Holocaust Memorial Trust describes dehumanisation as the fourth of the ten steps towards genocide; the fifth is organisation and the sixth is polarisation, all echoed in the Weston-super-Mare demonstration.

At last year's Holocaust Memorial Day in Dorchester, I was asked to be a speaker and took, as a visual aid, the skull of a goat (including horns) and suggested that one of people's favourite scapegoats today was Gypsies and Travellers, and I urged people to recognise the temptation to blame others when all is not going well in their own lives. My experience of living in community has taught me how groups of people love to have a scapegoat. Time and again at Pilsdon, and even at the gentler Hilfield Friary, someone has become the community scapegoat. This person will be the one nearly everybody complains about and many find difficult; they become a convenient person on which to dump all our unresolved fear and discontent. Sometimes at Pilsdon it would be a young person, sometimes someone foreign, a person with Asperger's who was struggling to communicate, a person with a disability, or a posh former public school boy. It didn't seem to matter who it was, there had to be someone to blame and shoulder the burden of all our inadequacies. As community members, we would work hard to process our own tendencies to dump our stuff on others and strongly defend the person scapegoated, but it never completely stopped rising to the surface. After a while, as each scapegoat left, we began to wonder who would take on the role next.

At Hilfield, you can judge the spiritual health of the community by noticing people's individual and collective desire to find a scapegoat. Some people arrive who, in a strange way, seem to feel comfortable in the role of scapegoat – they almost willingly walk into the role as it's a familiar coat they are used to wearing. When you get to know those who self-select themselves as scapegoat, and hear their story, you find they were the one in the family who were blamed when things went wrong, they were the person who was picked on at school and then later at work. It's shocking when people normalise being a victim, but still more disturbing when a community or nation uses an individual or a group to find a simple solution to their individual or collective woes by blaming another.

We had a rather eccentric, socially clumsy, but hugely willing community member at Hilfield who at times became a figure of fun and ridicule. He became for me a touchstone of the community's health. When the community was functioning well he seemed to thrive on the encouragement that came from others. When we had less generous and self-aware community members he'd often become the butt of numerous jokes and people would roll their eyes at meetings when he spoke; it was as though he'd become a target for our collective failures.

Scapegoating, I think, is best challenged by naming it: calling out 'Pikey' jokes as racism against Gypsies; challenging language that describes 'swarms of refugees' waiting to 'invade' our country; gently asking people complaining about immigration if they've ever met a refugee or heard about the violence in the country they're fleeing; or telling the Islamophobe about a Muslim friend; perhaps singing the praises of the person another is criticising and wondering out loud how it feels to be in the skin of the person targeted. The positive story about a group of Romany Gypsies who raised £6000 for a nursing home that provided terminal care for one of their community in Darlington, if told in the local press, challenges the more common stories of Travellers 'invading' a neighbourhood. Perhaps the reason it's easier to sell negative news is because the tendency to blame another apparently worse than ourselves allows us to feel better about ourselves. If we can slough off some of our unresolved fear and anger onto another group, it saves us having to do the harder work of processing our own difficult feelings. It was the local media who whipped up antagonism against the proposed move-on house in Dorchester, deliberately playing on people's fear and turning it to anger. What challenged and demolished people's fears was an open encounter with members of the community, through our willingness to risk crossing the divide between us and them.

EXPLORING OUR SHADOW SIDE

Carl Jung described these difficult and often unexamined parts of our psyche as our 'shadow' side, but far from urging us to deny or repress these hidden parts of ourselves, he urged us to befriend our fears. He saw confronting our shadow side as an opportunity for the release of much pent-up energy, and the possibility for real growth. Jung (1938, p.140) says:

> If you imagine someone who is brave enough to withdraw all his projections, then you get an individual who is conscious of a pretty thick shadow. Such a person has saddled himself with new problems and conflicts. He has become a serious problem to himself, as he is now unable to say that they do this or that, they are wrong, they must be fought against... Such a man knows that whatever is wrong in the world is in himself, and if he only learns to deal with his own shadow he has done something real for the world. He has succeeded in shouldering at least an infinitesimal part of the gigantic, unresolved problems of our day.

Jung described our shadow as 90 per cent pure gold, and if we have the courage to recognise and befriend it, it can be hugely empowering. In a similar vein, the Dalai Lama talks of how 'our enemy is our secret teacher'.

When we fail to examine our own shadow feelings of revulsion and distaste, but project them onto others, we can too easily get into an unhelpful cycle of condemnation of others. If we fail to look at our shadow side, we also do damage to ourselves. A further temptation with difficult feelings, rather than blaming others for them, is to suppress them and look for compensating good feelings or highs. This flight from our shadow can all too easily lead to addiction to the compensating distraction which, because it is based on a fundamental denial and failure to integrate our true feelings, never truly satisfies. Thus, it's easy to fall into a cycle of addiction. Better to face up to our fears, sit with the discomfort and work through them, as that's a more likely route towards inner freedom.

In 2010, I spent three months in Israel/Palestine, as part of the World Council of Churches Ecumenical Accompaniment Programme in Palestine and Israel, and just before I went out, I attended a training session, part of which involved a woman on the same programme, who had recently returned, giving a PowerPoint presentation of her experiences. Her presentation was shrill and loud in its condemnation of the iniquities of the Israeli occupation of the West Bank. It seemed so polarised and lacking in balance that I felt it would alienate all but the diehard pro-Palestinian lobby, and I vowed that I'd never give such an unbalanced talk nor allow myself to be polarised as so many are by the Israeli/Palestinian conflict.

Four months later, after having completed three months, immersed in the life of a Palestinian village, I was returning home and crossing Waterloo Bridge. On the pavement in front of me was an Orthodox Jewish couple with a child hanging onto the side of a pushchair and a baby inside it. The mother wore a headscarf and the father and son kippahs, denoting them as Orthodox Jews. I had never met the family, but found myself having such profound feelings of revulsion for them that I crossed over the road as I couldn't bear to be near them. I noticed my feelings of revulsion turning to despair.

What had just happened to me was what I'd sworn never would. I too, Jonathan Herbert, usually the 'peacemaker' who always sees everyone's point of view, had become polarised, projecting my anger at the injustice of the Israeli occupation on an innocent Jewish family. What was I to do? My intuition was to sit with the feelings and try and process them once I got home, and pray for enlightenment. So that's what I did. It was hard. That experience of revulsion towards the family made me feel dirty and ashamed.

Two weeks later, I was looking at some photographs I'd taken whilst in the West Bank, and a picture I'd taken early one evening outside an Israeli settlement caught my eye. In the distance, the low sun was reflecting off newly built whitewashed houses. In the foreground was an ancient olive grove, and linking the two was a dusty path on which I'd photographed my long shadow stretching out in front. As I looked at it again, I focused on the shadow and began to understand what had been happening to me, and to the Jewish people for centuries.

I began to understand that my reaction came from my shadow side. I knew my extreme reaction to the couple on the bridge was my anger at the cruelty of the occupation of the West Bank by the Israeli military, which I'd experienced so recently, being projected onto this innocent couple. I knew I could work on this and not be consumed by it and use it to campaign for peace and justice in the region in the future. The greater gift, though, was my realisation that the Jewish people had been living under the shadow of persecution for over 3000 years, with the shadow of the Holocaust and genocide still powerfully present in the psyche of the Israeli state. Immediately I understood why, whilst in conversation with an Israeli, if you failed to fully endorse state policy or even mildly criticise it, someone you thought of as highly educated and fairly liberal in their outlook would suddenly be standing up and shouting at you.

The polarisation and anger I'd felt suddenly dispersed and was replaced with an intense feeling of compassion for myself and the Jewish people. I no longer felt split and had moved to a place where I could give a more balanced presentation of my experience, whilst still being an advocate for an end to the military occupation of the

West Bank and the numerous breaches of the human rights of so many Palestinians. I also felt internally robust enough to refute allegations that I was being anti-Semitic when I gently pointed out some of the human suffering caused by over 50 years of military occupation. My shadow indeed had been my greatest teacher. Like the shadow in that photograph or our shadow on a sunny day, our shadow side always travels with us, but too often it goes unnoticed and unowned, which can lead us to project our own discomfort onto others. I'm slowly learning that noticing how my shadow accompanies me and learning to notice and befriend it allows me to better accompany others.

POLARISATION

Another picture I sometimes show is a picture I took at a checkpoint for Palestinian workers crossing into Israel. It shows a watchtower, barbed wire fences and a queue of over 4000 dispirited-looking men wrapped up against the cold in the grey light preceding dawn. When I ask people what it reminds them of, they will almost always say Jews outside a concentration camp. It's a chilling reply that points to the irony that a people once themselves so oppressed are now using some of the methods of their oppressors.

Two mornings a week, one of my tasks as an Ecumenical Accompanier in Israel/Palestine was to get up at 3 a.m. in order to be at that checkpoint, where thousands of married Palestinian men between the ages of 35 and 60 would be queueing up to go to work across the security barrier between the West Bank and where construction work was in Israel. It was the worst part of the whole programme, partly because of the early rising but more so because of the long queues of defeated-looking men, waiting sometimes three or four hours to pass through the turnstiles, have their passes checked, be scanned for weapons and have fingerprints checked. The deliberate slowness of the private security firm who ran the Qalqilya checkpoint seemed designed to humiliate and demean those desperate for work. The only bright point of those early mornings was occasionally meeting the women of Machsom Watch, an Israeli human rights organisation, who'd also be checking that the Israeli army and the security firm were treating people with dignity. These courageous women were determined to challenge the worst abuses of the occupation and, like us, through their presence, stand in solidarity with the Palestinian people.

Israel began building a security barrier to protect Israeli settlements from attacks and suicide bombings in 2002 and, Palestinians would say, to annexe large parts of the West Bank which now have effectively become part of Israel. The barrier runs for over 700 kilometres and snakes deep into the West Bank. The Palestinians call it 'the Wall', but for most of its length it's two electrified fences with ditches and barbed wire each side and a road for military vehicles to speed up and down in the middle. Only in urban areas like Jerusalem and Bethlehem does it turn into an eight-metre-high wall. In the programme, we called it the separation barrier; others called it the 'apartheid' wall, as its purpose was to separate two peoples. Towns like Qalqilya had formerly been places where many Israeli Jews would come and shop and mix freely with the Palestinian population, but the building of the concrete walls here had meant many local businesses had gone bust; the main road into Israel was becoming overgrown and ended abruptly at the wall.

The building of walls, be it in Israel/Palestine, in Berlin, Belfast or along the Mexican/USA border, seems to be a metaphor for the breakdown of human relationships and aids division and polarisation. If you never get to meet your neighbours, it becomes much easier to stereotype them as alien and dangerous. Our othering only lasts as long as we resist truly meeting the 'enemy', but walls reinforce our defensiveness and distrust and, by separating people, create strangers. Sadly, for Palestinians, because of the separation barrier, the only Jewish people they met were usually soldiers, police or security guards imposing the occupation at gunpoint, so it became easy for them to caricature all Israelis as the brutal oppressor. Likewise, for the young Israeli conscripts manning crossing points, any Palestinian was a potential terrorist. So it was easy for fear and loathing to build on both sides of the wall.

The wisdom of the Ecumenical Accompaniment Programme in Israel/Palestine, of which I was part, was that it encouraged the internationals who engaged in it to live and walk alongside Palestinians and Israelis. I spent most of those months living in the village of Jayous, getting to know many of the villagers and their stories by simply spending time on the streets and accepting numerous invitations into people's homes. The village was entirely Muslim but greeted our team of four from churches in Sweden, Norway, Canada and the UK with typically generous Palestinian hospitality. Many couldn't really understand why we would leave our families, children and grandchildren to stand in solidarity with them, but they were immensely grateful.

Our landlord in Jayous was Abu Assam, the head of a leading family in the village, and he was a passionate campaigner for a just peace in the region. He was a leading figure in the 'Stop the Wall' coalition, had been on numerous protests about the building of the separation barrier, and had taken the Israeli government to court over the loss of his land to the nearby settlement and won part of it back. Once the wall had been built he could only get to his land with a permit which would sometimes be revoked for months at a time by the military administration. Each day he would queue up at the checkpoint on his elderly Massey Ferguson tractor to have several hours tending his olive trees and polytunnel. He'd spent time in jail for his beliefs but was determined to build peace by engaging with Israelis whenever he could. He would say how saddened he was when he heard of the death or injury of an Israeli soldier: 'I too am a father with sons, and can imagine the pain of the parents of a dead soldier.' Abu Assam refused to give in to the temptation of othering – he always saw the person first and used hospitality as a way to build friendship, accompany others, break down difference and build bridges.

BUILDING BRIDGES

Hope sometimes needs to come from outside, as well as from within communities. In my five years as a vicar on the post-war Beechdale council estate in Walsall, I sought to embody and generate hope through my work with the church and community there. When I arrived, the place was referred to in the press as 'the troubled Beechdale estate.' It was as though the whole estate had been written off and was a 'no go' area for those outside it, and the people of the estate had a very poor image of themselves. Arriving for my interview and to look round the parish, I remember several of the church people saying, 'We're not that bad, you know,' and almost begging me to come to a job that had been vacant for nearly two years and nobody had applied for. I actually liked the look of the place, abandoned as its people felt. I could see it was a distinct community; it was bounded on all sides by a motorway, railway line and a canal. It had a distinct centre with a row of shops, library, housing office, working man's club, church and the vicar's house all on four sides of Stephenson Square. Many people had lived there all their lives since its building in the 1950s, and many of their children and grandchildren were still living there. There were high rates of unemployment and low wages for those in work, low educational achievement and poor health compared to the leafier suburbs, and lots of crime and anti-social behaviour, but the thing that shocked me most about the place after coming from a much rougher but far more vibrant community in Liverpool was the persistently negative attitude of the people. Individuals there seemed to have little self-worth and seemed to have embraced the local media's gloomy view of Beechdale. I felt strongly that one of my major tasks there was to challenge their negative self-image and help reassert a new pride in the estate. I determined to use every opportunity to speak positively about the place and encourage people to celebrate the very close-knit nature of community. Though an outsider, I sensed that the way to be part of transforming the place was to seek to build trust by accompanying the community through the simple act of living there.

As the local vicar I was the only professional person who lived on the estate, which gave me the opportunity to bring something new to the community whilst also living in solidarity with the people there. All the other professionals working in the health centre, housing office, schools and the community centre left work at 3 p.m. on a Friday, when there would be a procession of smart cars leaving the estate. This exodus seemed to symbolise the 'them and us' divide and why places like Beechdale feel abandoned. Across the country, this divide between local residents and public servants seems to have been exacerbated by attempts to introduce accountability to those working in public services, which has led to a culture of targets and quantifiable outcomes, which all have to be recorded. The strong emphasis on keeping people safe, aimed at protecting children and vulnerable adults, which is, of course, vitally important, has also led to a growth in deskbound paperwork, and growing bureaucracy has further cut down on the time workers have to meet people and, crucially, build trust with local communities. For too many community workers, the office, rather than the street and people's homes, has become the place they spend most of their working lives, and they thus become distanced from the people they are paid to engage with.

The local bond seems to be being gradually severed as society becomes more fragmented. Houses where the local policeman lived were sold off years ago, and a whole rota of nameless officers will occasionally patrol places like Beechdale by car. Thirty years ago you would know your local bank manager, who had often been in post for many years and they, in turn, would know you and be able to make very informed decisions about granting a loan or not. If you are lucky enough to see someone in a bank today, it'll be a newly appointed business manager using a clever algorithm to assess how the bank might profit from you.

One of the great strengths of the Church of England's parish system is that vicars are expected to live in the place they work. By going to live on the Beechdale estate, I was challenging this dualism of working in one place and living in another. I was undoubtedly an outsider and was easily recognisable by the way I talked and dressed.

Once I'd led a couple of assemblies at the two primary schools, taken a big community funeral and visited the working men's club on a Saturday night, half the community knew or knew of me. After a few weeks into life on the estate, I recognised that not only were there divisions between Beechdale and the wider world but there was also a clear division between those who went to St Chad's Church, where I was vicar, and the rest of the estate. The church seemed to have little involvement with the community, and nobody outside the small congregation much used the church buildings. Slowly we began to reverse this by encouraging members of the church to become involved in community activities, such as a credit union, an arts forum and a gospel choir, and also in making the church buildings more available for people to use, so the church, rather than being separate from, began to accompany the community.

By regularly visiting the local pubs and social club, I began to break down divisions between church and community. One evening in the social club, I was approached to do a home baptism, as the family didn't want their children baptised in church but at their former council house, which they'd recently refurbished and dug a swimming pool in the garden. I said I'd be happy to, as long as I could bless the house and baptise the children in the pool. So we did, with over 200 people packed into the garden around the pool, far more than would have come to the church. As I performed the ceremony immersed in the water of the pool, I felt a real washing away of the barriers between those inside and outside the church.

CHALLENGING PREJUDICE

Life wasn't easy for a lot of people on the estate and part of the community's shadow came out in the overt racism of a significant minority of people there. The estate of 10,000 people, in spite of being in Walsall, one of the most culturally diverse towns in Britain, was almost exclusively white, with only a couple of dual heritage families and a Jamaican man nicknamed 'Chalky'. Whilst I was there, the council were preparing to let a property to an Asian family who'd been seen viewing the house, but the day before they moved in every window at the front of the house was smashed in so they never did. The estate had been a traditional recruiting ground for the National Front, who by the 1990s had given way to the British National Party (BNP). On two occasions we also had the front windows of our house smashed in by bricks, once after hosting Sikh friends, then one evening after inviting a black gospel choir to sing in the church. Using an alias, I managed to get on the BNP mailing list and was able to warn local anti-fascist organisations about planned meetings and demonstrations which they were often able to disrupt.

One way of challenging this racism was to encourage people from the estate to meet people from different cultural backgrounds. We employed two huge dreadlocked Rastafarians to run drumming workshops, leading up to our annual carnival procession, with some of the youth from the estate. These men were so macho and assertive and had such 'street cred' that in spite of their colour, they instantly gained the respect and admiration of a group of the most disruptive teenagers, and began to challenge some of their assumptions. One of the two particularly impressed the youngsters by eating a whole roast chicken in a matter of seconds. They were expensive to hire but worth every penny for the quality of their percussive work and the way they engaged some of our most disaffected youth. It's those real encounters with others that begin to allow people to dismantle their prejudices. When you've spent a great day making your own drums and beating out rhythms, it gets harder to write people off as no good or alien.

Our congregation also joined a broad-based community organising group called 'Citizens', an organisation built up of faith groups and secular bodies to bring about change across the former industrial area around Walsall, Wolverhampton and Dudley. For the first time, people from Beechdale were meeting Muslims, Hindus, and Sikhs and planning how to challenge those in power to work and engage with local communities to bring about lasting change on a series of local issues. To be sitting in the office of the local police chief superintendent with two women leaders from Beechdale, a Roman Catholic priest from Wolverhampton, Herminder Singh from a Walsall gurdwara and Mr Patel from the main Hindu temple in the town, and demanding the reinstatement of community policing on Beechdale was hugely empowering for the women from the estate. Community organising was born in Chicago in the 1950s out of the work of Saul Alinsky, who aimed to create a broad-based, grassroots organisation to bring about change amongst the communities most blighted by poverty and those that felt most alienated by the institutions of power in government and industry. Barrack Obama was trained as an organiser in Chicago and used many of Alinsky's methods to build up a broad coalition of support for his 2007 election campaign.

On the Beechdale estate, community organising was transformative for the people who became involved with it, and it diminished the divide between local people and those in positions of power, as it gave people the confidence to challenge the council, the police and other organisations to work in meaningful partnership, rather than in a top-down way. It also opened people's eyes to the richness and vibrancy of other faith traditions, and began to break down prejudices and fears people had about those from different cultures. The fundamental building block of community organising is the 'relational meeting'; this is a one-to-one meeting with other members of the coalition. Constant one-to-one meetings between members of the coalition build trust and a sense of belonging to the organisation, and allow people to listen to each other's concerns and identify key issues for the organisation to act upon. These relational meetings are what I would describe as accompaniment, and this making time to be with each other was the vital part of building an organisation for change and overcoming people's sense of powerlessness.

Whilst community organising was beginning on the estate, we were also putting together a community play called *Daledreams*, which told the story Beechdale from its earliest years up until the 1990s. The first story it told was 'Vera's Story'. Vera moved to what was then known as Gypsy Lane Estate in the 1950s. Before houses had been built, it had been a traditional stopping place for Romany Gypsies, hence the name. Vera's family in West Yorkshire had taken in a refugee family from the Spanish Civil War in the 1930s, so when the Gypsies came calling and asked for water, Vera knew it was her duty to help. She befriended a large Gypsy family, but was criticised and shunned by her neighbours for many years afterwards. Her reaching out to the family across the traditional divide, between nomadic and settled people, in spite of the poisonous tongues of her neighbours, who in *Daledreams* became a chorus of disapproval, was portrayed in the play as a noble act, and for her vindicated the stand she'd taken 40 years before.

Sadly, the anti-Gypsy feelings of the 1950s don't seem to have changed much compared to the progress made in fighting racism against other ethnic groups. Some call anti-Traveller prejudice the last acceptable form of racism. There is fear and suspicion on both sides between Travellers and the settled community, which means it is rare for both communities to have meaningful encounters. Since the Egyptians Act of 1530 (people wrongly assumed that the Romany people had come from Egypt, hence the name Gypsies), each century has seen the introduction of anti-Gypsy legislation. As recently as 2015, planning guidance to local authorities was given that required that those of a nomadic way of life would have to prove they were still travelling in order to qualify for planning permission so they could settle. As most Travellers can no longer travel, due to the almost total elimination of traditional stopping places through housing developments, industrial sites, the establishment of country parks and so on, many Traveller activists say it is legislation that is seeking to define them out of existence.

In 2015 I attended a parish council meeting in a nearby village that had been alerted to the fact that a Romany man and his immediate family had been living on a piece of land he'd bought on the outskirts of the village, because he'd applied for planning permission to settle there. The village of Frampton only has about 300 residents, but most of them were there that night. I'd been tipped off about the meeting so knew what to expect. Unlike the Pilsdon public meeting mentioned earlier, this meeting was not well run, nor did it have any balance nor, it seemed to me, to have much factual content. It was full of hyperbole about the village being overrun by wild and lawless strangers. There could be as many as 70 pitches in the field with hundreds of Gypsies taking over the village. What about the local school and shops, how would they cope? There already had been a major crime wave (somebody had had a lawn mower stolen from a shed) and there was a danger of dogs and wild horses being out of control. I listened for about an hour to a litany of complaints and exaggeration based on fear and ignorance, and feeling rather fearful and isolated, I put my hand up to speak. I attempted to correct some of their factual inaccuracies and told them that Gypsies had probably been stopping by their village for a number of centuries and certainly the Gypsy family in question had long associations with the area, far longer than most people there, many who'd retired to the village from outside the county. To loud shouts of disapproval, I suggested they go and befriend the Romany family, as they were likely to get planning permission on appeal and would be their neighbours for years to come.

As I left, a couple of people from the local church came out to me hugely embarrassed by their stance, and trying to justify their position. I wish I'd stayed and talked with them, but I was hungry, and had had a bellyful of their prejudice, and was just too tired to relate well with them.

Part of my role as chaplain to Gypsies and Travellers in Dorset and Wiltshire is to be an advocate for Travellers, and that means seeking opportunities to engage with people like those in Frampton, and trying to dispel some of their fear and ignorance. By spending time with Travellers, I also try to act as a bridge between them and the settled community, which for good reason they have little trust in. I know how inbuilt the distrust and fear of nomadic people is in society as a whole, as I discovered the first few times I visited Traveller sites, and gauged my own fear and anxiety. I had to overcome the fantasy that I'd be attacked or abused, my vehicle stolen, or I'd have the dogs set on me. Instead, I was greeted with respect, courtesy and reserve, from a community that has been so much maligned and denigrated in the public imagination.

In my role as chaplain it's been wonderful to open people's minds to the richness of the heritage of Romany Gypsies and Irish Travellers and let people know the many challenges their communities face. Leading cultural awareness training with Romany friends has been an important step in dismantling the wall of hostility between the settled community and Travellers. The most important part of this training is always when Travellers tell their own story, letting people know about the joys and sorrows of living in an extended family and the prejudice they have to negotiate each day. When people meet real people rather than the 'other' of their imagination, their prejudices are nearly always confounded and bridges built.

Kushti Bok, the Dorset-based campaigning group of Gypsies and Travellers, runs a project called 'Positive Stories', where Travellers collect the stories of other Travellers, which are then shared on social media and will eventually be collected for a book and film. The aim of the project is to give the communities pride in their heritage and break down prejudice in the wider community by sharing real human stories that show the cost of the continued vilification of Traveller communities. Facts and statistics about the grave inequalities Travellers face in terms of poor educational achievement and poor physical and mental health are shocking and show a huge need, but what will really bring about change is when people's personal testimonies are heard. Some of the Traveller activists I know get frustrated at the slow pace of change and the intense political opposition to Travellers, but I always encourage them to keep the faith and have hope. Change so often comes about through the continued and focused actions of small dedicated numbers of people that slowly build into a movement. Who would have thought in the early 1980s that apartheid in South Africa would be dismantled and Mandela elected as president in 1994, or that the rights and general acceptance that members of the LGBT community enjoy today could have been achieved so quickly (although there is still a long way to go before they are fully accepted)? Historically, prejudice has been overcome by people being prepared to cross the divide, name it, challenge it and let their voices be heard, and by building networks of solidarity and mutual support.

BUILDING SOLIDARITY

My education as an activist started in Liverpool, where I had my first job in the church on the Tower Hill estate, built in the 1970s as an overspill estate from the 1950s town of Kirkby. The locals referred to it as 'Beirut', as there were a whole number of empty and burnt-out buildings, few amenities, high rates of unemployment, and a huge number of young people using heroin, which meant there were frequent burglaries and theft from vehicles. Blighted as the community was, there was an incredible vigour and vibrancy to the people, who had a strong sense of solidarity, and many had a passion to seek redress for the economic and social ills that they saw as having been caused by the policies of successive governments. The estate had been built through the collusion of the then leader of Knowsley Borough Council and a builder who had built substandard homes in the smallest possible area, with little regulation. The houses, instead of being back to back, were back to front with walkways instead of roads between them, which made everywhere seem congested. The roads that were there weren't even given names – we lived at F25 Heathfield. The leader of the council and the builder both went to prison charged with corruption. The local people said, 'They got two years, we got life.'

It was a big culture shock for me coming to live on a council estate after two years living in the shadow of Lincoln Cathedral, where I was at college. I'd lived four years in inner-city St Pauls in Bristol, but this place was different, and here I was very obviously an outsider in a close-knit community. We protected our council house by getting two Great Danes, who were gentle with our young children but were reassuringly large with an impressive bark. In my first week there, I took the funeral of the daughter of the man who ran the local boxing club and lived opposite and, once we became friends, any fear of being broken into disappeared. I was uncertain, though, where to place my energy, but the people I found most engaging were the local activists, many of whom had been barred from the local Labour Party. They'd formed the Kirkby Unemployed Workers Centre which specialised in giving people advice about their housing and state benefits, and ran an arts project for women coming off drugs, a Theatre in Education company and a low-cost café. It was a great place to hang out and learn about what most affected the local communities and be part of some radical solutions to the poverty that was so endemic.

The word that seemed to sum up the centre and the community as a whole was 'solidarity', and I sensed that if I was to thrive in this community, I had to clearly show them I was on their side and cross over from my rather privileged and protected status as a vicar, step out of a purely religious and set-apart role and risk becoming involved politically. I joined the Tower Hill Labour Party and was soon appointed membership secretary; because of the imposition of the Poll Tax, a hugely unjust form of local taxation which was paid at the same rate regardless of wealth and property ownership, membership grew rapidly.

I, like many others, decided that this tax, a tax that was levied at a flat rate whatever your income or capital assets, was profoundly unjust and needed to be challenged. Like many others, I decided that the best way to defeat the tax was to refuse to pay it. This brought me into direct conflict with my team rector, who instructed me to pay it, arguing that, as a Christian, it was never right to break the law. I argued otherwise, taking the view that it was a matter of conscience, and I was not prepared to support a system of taxation that allowed a wealthy landowner with multiple properties to pay the same rate of tax as a poorly paid labourer. I was then told by my boss that if I didn't pay it, my chances of preferment in the church would be seriously damaged. I had to ask him what he meant by preferment.

'Your career in the church will be irreparably damaged.'

'Oh,' I replied angrily, 'I didn't come into the church for a career, for me it's a vocation, and part of my vocation is to stand with the poor and marginalised, which right here, right now means refusing to pay this tax like everyone else on Tower Hill!'

It was great a few weeks later to be queuing up, accompanying my parishioners in a line of hundreds outside the Magistrates' Court, and see the delight in people's faces when they saw the vicar in the same queue as them. I never had to choose whether to go to prison with them or not because, as a result of the massive campaign of non-payment, the Poll Tax was defeated a few weeks later. In a way, though, it was costly for me as a few months later I was asked to leave the Diocese of Liverpool when my initial contract came to an end.

I was sorry to leave such a vibrant community, and for several years afterwards felt angry that an injustice had been done to me for not toeing the line and that my motives were misunderstood. What really angered me was that I was accused of having no spiritual life, being shallow and being a flag-waving rebel. My protest about the Poll Tax and other injustices grew directly out of prayerful reflection and conviction that, if Christianity was to mean anything to the people of Tower Hill, people in the church needed to be seen to be on the side of the poor and marginalised. These days, I'd know how to manage my conflict with the church, and also my own inner conflicts, better. Then, I think I was a little quick to give into the temptation to take sides and blame those in authority. Today, I would be more interested in building relationships with the church hierarchy, allowing me to challenge them but from a place of mutual respect. It was easier to put myself in the position of self-righteous victim rather than doing the hard work of reflecting on my own needs and motivations and the profound pressures to conform placed on those in authority in the church.

Solidarity is all well and good but, if conflicts are to be transformed and if we are to recognise our shadow sides and our own part in every conflict, then we have to be prepared to work hard at it and forgo the luxury of simply taking sides and blaming the other. Accompaniment has taught me that to dismantle notions of otherness and break down difference there are no short cuts and it's all about building relationships. Fear and suspicion are only broken down by real engagement and the often painstaking process of building trust, being prepared to stay with our own discomfort, and gently, firmly and consistently challenging local and institutional prejudice.

In the next chapter, I shall begin to look at how the building of relationships is at the heart of breaking down conflict, enmity and division and is a vital step on the way to building peace.

6

MAKING PEACE
WITH OTHERS

CONFLICT

I awake in the middle of the night, a hand shaking my shoulder and a voice gently telling me, 'Wake up, there's soldiers and military vehicles outside,' and sure enough, I can feel the house vibrating to the throb of the vehicles. I quickly dress and step out into the garden compound, lit up by the lights of the Humvees and army jeeps in a convoy along the street. It's raining hard and there's been thunder, which is why the military chose this night. I open the gate onto the main street of Jayous to try to work out what's going on and immediately have an automatic gun pointed inches away from my belly. I instinctively raise my hands, like I did as a child playing Cowboys and Indians, look the young Israeli soldier in the eyes and with my arms still raised point to my head and say, 'International! International!' I ask him what's happening, and he waves a paper at me, tells me that I'm in a closed military zone and orders me to get back into the compound. I retreat into the garden but leave the door open so that I can observe what's going on. Quickly the engines are revved, the foot soldiers jump into the jeeps and as the convoy passes the house I count 13 vehicles. As soon as they leave I return to the street, where I'm joined by my Palestinian neighbours, who seem much less shocked than me. 'What's happened?' I ask, and they tell me there's been another raid on the village by the Israeli army, and several young men from Jayous will soon be in custody at the local barracks and then taken across the border to prison in Israel. It's a cool January night and the rain is relentless, so we go back into our houses and I say to my colleague David, 'Now I've seen the occupation,' and climb back into the comfort of my bed.

It's 2010, and I'm two weeks into living in the Palestinian village of Jayous on the West Bank, as part of the World Council of Churches EAPPI. We're a small international team of four: myself, David Pan from Canada (though 'made in Taiwan' as he likes to tell people), Sophie from Sweden and Ida from Norway.

The Ecumenical Accompaniment Programme, of which we were a part, began in 2002, in response to leaders of 12 Christian churches in Jerusalem writing to the World Council of Churches in 2000 at the height of the Israeli military crackdown of the Second Intifada, saying that they felt forgotten by the rest of the world churches, and asking that they come and see what was happening to them and let others know. The programme was born out of this and has, at its heart, three things: first, solidarity with Palestinian Christians and Israeli and Palestinian peace activists, second, the notion of protection by presence, and third, advocacy work once the accompaniers return home. I jumped at the chance to be part of the programme, as I found the idea of living alongside others, accompanying them for a short while in their daily lives, mixed with the notion of peacemaking in probably the world's most intractable conflict, strangely attractive.

The next day I'm up early walking to the agricultural crossing point, where the few Palestinian farmers in the village who have been issued with permits by the military queue up to show papers to soldiers at a checkpoint in the electrified fence, to get to their land across the separation barrier. The birds are singing, the air is clean and the light bright after the night's rain. I pass an ancient 500-year-old olive tree, turn the corner, look down the hill and see the separation barrier snaking its way through the hills. To the left is the Israeli settlement of Zufin, with the sun glinting off its whitewashed walls and lighting up its terracotta tiles, and to the right is the remainder of the village land not expropriated for the settlement. I spend the next 45 minutes counting 25 men, 6 donkeys and 12 sheep crossing over into the no man's land, where people go to tend their olive trees and polytunnels. The locals say they like it when we're at the checkpoint, as they get treated better by the soldiers when we're there.

On the way back, I stop at Mohammed's shop to buy food for breakfast, and he seems strangely subdued, not his usual welcoming and friendly self, so I ask him, 'What's wrong?'

'It's my son,' he says, 'He was taken last night,' and tears fill his eyes. The news hits me in the guts, as the previous evening I had been showing him pictures of my two sons. 'How would you feel', he says, 'if it was one of your sons that was taken?'

There's nothing I can say. I just stand there shaking my head. In the night, I had seen how the occupation worked; now, in the bright light of day, I was beginning to feel how it works. I stand a little longer in the shop, watching other customers come in, watching some get really angry when they hear the news and others console Mohammed with stories of when their children were taken, saying his son will eventually return. I force myself to stay a little longer, feeling the intense discomfort of this generous man's pain, trying to stand with him in some kind of solidarity, but desperately trying to think of something useful to do. I remember there's an Israeli group of lawyers who can find out which Israeli jail Palestinian prisoners get taken to, so I promise to try and find out and to come back to see how he is later.

My encounter was typical of so many meetings I had with people in the village whose sons were 'missing' in Israeli prisons. I asked people why they thought the army took their sons. Many said, 'Because they can.' Others said, 'To show they are in control,' and others, 'To persuade us to leave, but we never will.' Incarcerating young men in prison anywhere seems only to make things worse, and here it was a sure way of perpetuating conflict. Conflict everywhere continues and becomes inevitable where violence, mistrust and fear are contained in a narrative that says we're so different we can never live together. The challenge for us as accompaniers in Israel/Palestine was to try to gently and humbly challenge the old and angry voices of despair and polarisation, by being present in the midst of the conflict and offering an alternative narrative. The gift that accompaniment can bring to any conflict is the refusal to give in to the temptation to quickly take sides and rush to judgement, but to begin where people are. Peace comes through the long-term building of relationships on the ground and accompaniment builds these by the practice of simply being present, listening to people sharing their lives, and not trying to impose solutions or, like the Israeli army, control things.

CONFLICT

When somebody threatens or criticises one of your children the reaction is usually visceral, and I had some inkling of how Mohammed felt. Some months earlier, at Pilsdon, I'd experienced a violent reaction to someone threatening my eldest son. There was a man called Rodney, who'd been staying with us for a few weeks, who was a well travelled, well read and gently spoken, with a long flowing grey beard that went with his esoteric musings. He described himself as bi-polar and wanted to stay in a place that would ground him in reality and give him a strong structure and regular routine. He seemed like he would be a good fit, so we said yes to him coming to live in the community, outlining what I called the 'Magnificent Seven' boundaries we asked people not to cross. One of these was no violence or threatening behaviour, to which he replied that he was a pacifist but did sometimes have a propensity to shout at people. I told him this would not be acceptable, as shouting can be very intimidating for some people.

A couple of weeks into his time with us, I heard someone shouting in the yard. It was a new voice I didn't recognise, and as I walked out, I saw it was the mild-mannered Rodney, his voice transformed into that of a foul-mouthed London docker, bawling out one of our guests. I quickly stepped in and defused the situation, and Rodney rapidly calmed down and apologised immediately. I reminded him of our culture of no violence or intimidation and he agreed to abide by it. Sadly, it happened again and I gave him a final warning.

A couple of weeks later, I heard shouting from across the field and my stomach tightened as I ran towards it, recognising Rodney's voice and what I thought was the voice of our neighbour, Ian. I ran quickly, knowing that Ian, who ran a car breakers yard, had a short temper, was a tough no-nonsense guy and would be tempted to punch Rodney. I ran into the yard, only to see Rodney standing toe to toe with my 20-year-old son Ben, who was working breaking cars for Ian. I ran between them, I thought to make the peace, but suddenly I was shouting at Rodney and noticed my hand, as if acting on its own, raised to hit Rodney. Ian quickly jumped between us and dragged me away laughing, remembering times I had had to pacify him. My anger was gone, quick as Rodney's. We both apologised, and I quickly changed role from protective parent to leader of the community and sadly confirmed with Rod that he had to leave Pilsdon. Here was a boundary I needed to hold.

He left within the hour, and there was a collective sigh of relief in the community, as people had been anxiously waiting for his next explosion. I knew I'd made the right decision but was left with much to reflect on. For Rodney, it was the third bout of shouting in three weeks; for me it was the third time I'd shouted at somebody in 12 years. Conflict is an inevitable part of life and, though never easy, I'm learning it's always better to address it rather than ignore it or run away from it. As I ran across that field to confront the shouting I was hearing, I was full of dread but knew it was better to be there and take responsibility than pretend it wasn't happening. Too often, conflict escalates because people hope it'll go away or don't want to accept their own part in it and choose to blame others. We can't always fix things or resolve the fight immediately, as I wasn't able to with Rod, but by being prepared to take the risk of entering into it, the conflict did reach some kind of resolution.

As with Rodney, part of our role as accompaniers on the West Bank was to be with people in the midst of conflict, not turn a blind eye to it in order to avoid it, which is such a temptation. Sometimes our presence prevented conflict escalating; sometimes we were powerless to prevent it, but even then, it felt important to witness it, reflect on it later, and tell others back home the reality of facts on the ground and how a just peace might come about.

Given how closely people lived together in the community at Pilsdon and the amount of pain and frustration people lived with, it was remarkable that there was seldom a raised voice in the community. This was largely due to the culture of acceptance and love that we tried to nurture. If someone swore, we'd gently remind them there were children around, if there was any hint of bullying, we'd seek to address it, or if people had disagreements, we'd quickly encourage people to find a solution. Sometimes, though, two people would seriously fall out and when this happened we tried mediation. This took time, as the process I used was to get each of the protagonists to sit down separately with me, and I'd listen to their individual account of what was causing the conflict, and then, if they were willing to undergo the mediation, the three of us would sit down together. Each would listen to the other without interruption and then they would say what they had heard the other say. Then we would work towards resolution. So often, the ability to be honest and show a little vulnerability with the other led to major shifts in perception. When people really listened to each other in this way, anger and fear could quickly dissipate and be replaced by the beginnings of trust. I was always deeply moved when I saw people risk lowering their defences and talk about their real feelings, and the power this had to break down the defended parts of the other person. It was always hard work, and costly in terms of time and emotional energy, but when it worked, which it nearly always did, it felt like a really precious piece of accompaniment.

In 1984, Jo Berry's father, Sir Anthony Berry, was killed in the bombing of the Conservative Party Conference in Brighton, for which Patrick Magee was convicted and jailed for 16 years, finally being released after the Good Friday Agreement of 1997. Following his release, Jo decided that she had to meet him. She writes:

I wanted to meet Patrick to put a face to the enemy and see him as a real human being. At our first meeting I was terrified, but

I wanted to acknowledge the courage it had taken him to meet me. We talked with extraordinary intensity. I shared a lot about my father, while Patrick told me some of his story. (Cantacuzino 2015, p.96)

They carried on meeting and Patrick has supported Jo in her Building Bridges for Peace charity. This courage and willingness of Jo to be present to Patrick, and her determination to meet him as a fellow human being and walk into his story has been an inspiration to many others as a powerful step towards dismantling conflict.

Jo's encounter with Patrick, and any kind of mediation or attempts at conflict resolution, only work because, within the process, certain boundaries are agreed, such as listening to each other without interruption and treating one another with respect. Strong boundaries are necessary in all aspects of life for people to feel safe. I knew that by asking Rodney to leave Pilsdon, I was holding the boundary around unacceptable intimidation of others and maintaining peace in the community. There's a saying, 'Good fences make good neighbours,' which I'm sure is true, as long as it's a fence you can lean over and talk with your neighbour. When it's a six-foot wall, you tend not to get to know the person living next to you.

WALLS

Too often in our world, good boundaries are replaced by physical and metaphorical walls which isolate people from one another, and instead of building peace and security, promote fear and suspicion. Building a wall seems to be the ultimate symbol of polarisation and the opposite of a commitment to peace. So why do people do it? On one level perhaps it's about a desire to protect what we think we possess, to delineate what we own and hold dear and protect it from the other; it's about asserting our right to property. On an international scale, it's about asserting the sovereignty of the nation state, and that seems to be what has happened with Brexit in the UK. The fear of the free movement of people enshrined in the European Union's desire to promote trade across borders throughout the continent led to fears amongst many pro-Brexit voters that unrestricted migration to the UK threatened British jobs and would lead to great pressure on the health and education services. Strong anti-immigration rhetoric such as 'We want our country back' has led to the desire for the reassertion of national boundaries. In the USA, Donald Trump used the powerful symbol of a wall between the USA and Mexico, again to promote national sovereignty by restricting immigration, and rhetoric such as 'America First' to good effect in his 2016 election campaign. In the 1950s, Winston Churchill famously described an 'Iron Curtain' separating Eastern and Western Europe, which was literally made concrete in the 1960s with the building of the Berlin Wall and marked the beginning of the Cold War.

To build a wall is to provide people with a sense of security and seems to be a way of defining and protecting ourselves against the 'other'. It's a way of responding to our fear of the unknown 'other' and marking out ownership of our territory. The construction of walls, be they physical or in people's collective imagination, for me always reflects our failure to creatively respond to and make peace with those we fear, and prolongs conflict.

Recently, I was asked by a local vicar to advise a new local gamekeeper who had decided to assert his authority by banning some local Gypsies from shooting deer on the estate he managed. The previous gamekeeper had an informal agreement with the Gypsies that they could take the deer as long as they left the pheasants that were reared for the shoot. This arrangement had worked well until the new gamekeeper had decided to revoke the shooting rights. There'd been words and threats exchanged with the local Romanies, which involved guns being pointed. My suggestion was that the gamekeeper go back to the original agreement and bear in mind that Gypsies are nomadic, as are deer, and would have difficulty understanding how you can own creatures that know no boundaries themselves.

It's easy to see why people want to build walls and assert their ownership rights, particularly if they feel threatened and have wealth to protect, but the great danger of this is polarisation – once you're behind a wall, you lose your neighbour, who then becomes a stranger and can be seen as a threat, and the seeds of conflict begin to be sown.

The occupation of the West Bank began after the Six-Day War in 1967, and is still going on, each year seeing the chances of a viable Palestinian state diminishing as Israeli settlements continue to grow. I've always seen myself as something of a peacemaker, sometimes acting out the role of mediator with my ability to see and feel both sides of an argument. I knew how polarised people could get when talking about the Israeli–Palestinian conflict, and I was determined that that wasn't going to happen to me. I hated listening to the aggressive, fundamentalist hectoring of the Christian Zionist lobby, beating anyone who dared to criticise Israel's human rights record in the West Bank with the stick of anti-Semitism and quickly invoking the Holocaust to up the emotional ante. Almost as bad could be the shrill rhetoric of a leftist pro-Palestinian lobby with little understanding of how 3000 years of persecution of the Jewish people, along with the recent memory of the Holocaust, seems to shape modern Israel's understanding of itself.

The more I read about the suffering and injustices endured by the Palestinian population of Israel, the West Bank and Gaza, the more I knew that it would be deeply challenging to be there, but I was up for it. I have a deep love for the wisdom of the Torah, the Jewish prophets and the Psalms, which we use in our prayers four times a day at Hilfield Friary, and the immense intellectual and cultural legacy of the Jewish people, but I also know of my natural inclination to defend and take the side of the underdog (and make no mistake, this conflict is hugely asymmetrical, with the fourth most powerful army in the world usually matched against stone-throwing teenagers). I didn't want to jump to swift conclusions or take up a strongly defended position, as so many people do in our world, which only seems to perpetuate conflict and leads to the building of walls and sectarianism. Instead, I wanted to be with people, meet people from both sides, listen to what was happening on the ground, and understand the conflict by being present in the midst of it.

PRESENCE

The attraction for me of the Ecumenical Accompaniment Programme in Palestine and Israel was the idea that you went and lived in one place whilst meeting people on both sides of the conflict. We sought to offer protection by our presence and build relationships with the Israeli peace activists and the Palestinians we met. There was a lot of hanging around, talking to people on the street, drinking tea inside and outside people's houses, welcoming visitors to our house, playing football with the kids, chatting to Israeli soldiers at checkpoints, but above all we sought to understand people's lives by living and sharing village life. Ida and Sophie would tend to meet the women in the women's homes, and David and I did more talking to the men on the street. When a villager's son was arrested overnight, the next day we'd be round to pay our respects to the family and listen to their grief and anger. We'd also seek to meet up with Israelis working for peace and an end to the occupation when we crossed into Israel. We met with the Israeli human rights organisation Rabbis for Human Rights and the redoubtable Angela Godfrey, who works for the Israeli Committee Against House Demolitions, all seeking to work for a just and lasting peace. I also managed to befriend a secular Israeli settler who invited us to his house, where we marvelled at the plushness of his home and listened to what had led him to go and live on a settlement. Through becoming immersed in the lives of the people affected by the conflict, I began to have an understanding formed not by opinion, or even facts, but the lived experiences of the people I met.

Late one afternoon, I'd been drawn into a courtyard of a house near the separation barrier and was enjoying taking tea with a local Palestinian family. There'd been stone throwing by some village teenagers, with tear gas fired in response from the army earlier in the day, but all now seemed peaceful. We were sat in the shade of an olive tree, with a white dove cooing above us, perfect symbols of the peace we were feeling. Suddenly, we heard the whizz of something flying through the air, the clunking sound of metal on concrete, and somebody shouted 'Gas!' Immediately we were swathed in smoke, eyes streaming, lungs burning. We were quickly ushered into the house, issued with hastily split onions, which we held to our noses with the advice 'Don't rub your eyes.' Then we were hosed down with water back out in the courtyard. Once the gas had cleared, we walked home with throats burning but also with a deeper sense of solidarity with the people of the village. It felt like we'd gone through an initiation into the reality of village life. We really were accompanying the people there, fully present, sharing in all aspects of their lives.

Accompaniment through presence is a major part of the work of the charity Christian International Peace Services (CHIPS), and in 2011, I went out to Uganda to be part of a peacemaking team there. CHIPS, founded in 1966, taught that peace came through building up strong relationships of local trust. At the heart of its low-key, often hidden grassroots work was the building up of peacemaking teams of largely local people from both sides of a conflict and modelling how people could live peaceably together. CHIPS teams only go when they are invited by local communities, live at the heart of the conflict and, through experiencing it, understand it better. Central to CHIPSs way of working is the importance of being present to people and listening deeply to them in areas affected by violence. As they say in their website, 'We believe in taking sides. Both sides. We seek to understand everyone's perspective, and to build relationships' (CHIPS n.d.).

I met the founder of CHIPS, Roy Calvorcoressi, in October 2011 to explore doing a year's training in CHIPS methodology for peacemaking. We spent an inspiring couple of hours together and I left prepared to commit to the training. The following evening, I had a phone call from Roy asking me if I could go out to the CHIPS base in Uganda, as there were a few problems there he'd like me to help sort out. 'What about the year's training?' I asked.

'No need to worry about that,' he said. 'You seem to have plenty of relevant experience in being present to people – its presence, presence, presence that's all-important in peacemaking. Could you go next week, please?'

'No,' I heard myself saying, 'but I could go in three weeks' time.'

The next three weeks were filled with dread and anxiety, as I was briefed on the difficult situation at Okolonya CHIPS base in eastern Uganda. Money had been going missing, team members had not been living at the base but only turned up once a month to collect their salary, people had been sacked. Two new team members had been appointed along with me, and my task was to help rebuild the team. What I think I feared most was not getting sick 70 miles from the nearest hospital or being kidnapped by cattle raiders, but being caught in the middle of a conflict between different members of the team as the only European, and consequently feeling isolated. That, I think, is one of the main dangers and discomforts of all who seek to build peace in any conflict – the isolation which goes with not being clearly identified with one side, and not having the comfort that comes with taking up a simply defined and well-defended position.

Three weeks later, I was fighting my way onto a coach in Kampala and lucky to get a seat near the back alongside squawking chickens, skinny smiling children, and adults who were slightly bemused as to why a 'Mzungo' (white person) would want to go to Karamoja, the least developed, driest and most dangerous part of the country, where virtually no NGOs worked. As we entered Karamoja, the potholed, tarmacked road gave way to a dirt track, and where rain had ridged the road we were regularly bounced out of our seats. I climbed off the bus at Iriri, which felt like a town out of the Wild West, with just a few shacks with corrugated iron roofs, dust blowing everywhere, drunks hassling the only white man in town, but there, ready to greet me, was Simon Peter on a Honda 125 motorbike. 'We need to hurry,' he said. 'We need to get back before dark as there are armed men about.' We bought a sponge mattress, rolled it up, tied it to the back of the bike, and then I wedged myself behind Simon Peter and we set out into the bush along dirt roads and tracks to the base. We rode into Okolonya base, which was lit up by a huge welcoming fire, as the African night quickly descended onto us. It had only been a 150-mile journey but had taken nearly 12 hours.

The journey had been an induction into CHIPSs way of working. If I'd been in one of the numerous other NGOs in other parts of

Uganda, a driver would have picked me up from the airport in a smart four-by-four, air-conditioned Land Cruiser, and I'd have been whisked to my destination. CHIPSs way was that you used local transport, so you would understand how most people lived and meet ordinary people on the way. The only vehicles CHIPS had were one small motorbike and three sturdy, bone-shaking bicycles, for which we were always mending punctures. I lived in a mud hut with a grass roof, which I shared with dozens of rats. We pumped our water out of a borehole half a mile away, and we cooked over wood fires, which also served to light up the compound at night. We had a small solar panel to charge mobile phones, and strangely, the signal was far better than my faltering reception in Dorset. The simplicity of our life and its closeness to the lives of others who were beginning to resettle in the no man's land between Teso and Karamoja, where members of both tribes had been involved in cattle raiding and violent clashes for many years, enabled us to be aware of the effect of conflict in the region on people's everyday lives and gave CHIPS real credibility as a force for peace.

We were able to meet people where they were, be it sitting under a tree, pumping water from the borehole, helping build a house or collecting firewood. We built relationships by being prepared to live on the same level, in the same danger and eating the same food as our neighbours. This drew us closer to the people we lived amongst, helped us understand them and narrowed the differences between us, building a sense of shared experience. Bringing people from different sides of a conflict to work, receive training together and eat together were all effective ways CHIPS built trust and dispelled myths and rumours about the brutality of the 'other'.

CHIPS always engaged in very basic projects that were low cost and arising out of a local need: hand-dug wells, dam building, road making, training in agriculture. There was only one rule about all these projects and that was that they had to include an equal number of workers and trainees from both sides of the conflict. The CHIPS team at the base adhered to this; half our team of 12 were Karamajong and half were Iteso, with me the token white European thrown in for a bit of diversity. The biggest gain from all these joint enterprises wasn't the well or new road but the growth in co-operation and friendship between people of formerly opposing tribes. Once you've worked with people on a joint project, spent time with them, eaten with them, met their families and heard their story, it's much harder to polarise them or write off their tribe as brutal or stupid.

I did a lot of sitting round, under trees by day and the fire by night, learning to listen, first with my eyes observing body language and then with my ears as things were translated. I soon learnt that all these conversations went better when we had something to do with our hands. I joined in with shelling peanuts, chopping and drying cassava, sewing up old clothes, or the spoon making I introduced. It is this making time for each other, again, that is so important but that we rush past in the West, leading to so much loneliness, disconnection and conflict. I was learning that peacemaking begins with being present with the other, hearing their story and participating in local life to better understand the sources of conflict. Living alongside people can bring a lot of insight into the causes of conflict and can also help people find peaceful solutions.

After I'd completed my three months in Israel/Palestine, I was expected to give at least ten presentations about my experiences on the programme. Sometimes during the 30 or so presentations I made over the following two years, I began to see people in my audience and workshop begin to shift their once hard-held positions and this felt more significant and more important than anything I had achieved out in the West Bank. I concentrated in these talks on presenting my experience, what I had seen and heard and how it had affected me, as I believed that this was more likely to change people's understanding of the conflict than tub-thumping rhetoric or presenting well-reasoned arguments backed up by facts and statistics. Whenever I gave a presentation, my mind went back to a lunch with Afaf, a retired head teacher in the neighbouring village to Jayous. Sitting in the shade of an ancient olive tree on her land, we were picnicking with some of her friends and relations, and I was explaining that when I went home, I would focus on sharing my experiences when I met with groups. Like the good teacher she was, she said to them, 'Listen to what he said about sharing experience, *this is very important.*' What the accompaniment programme taught me is that for peacemaking to be effective, at its heart has to be a willingness to share and experience something of the lives of those at the centre of the conflict, reflect on it, be open to being changed, find peace in yourself, then share it with others.

My work as chaplain to Gypsies and Travellers could be described as being a bridge between the settled community and the nomadic community and involves communicating across a great historical divide of mutual suspicion and misinformation on both sides. In many ways, it's a peacemaking role, as feelings in the settled community, particularly, run high and the language used on social media and publicly by some MPs and local councillors is violent and incites hatred. One of the most challenging parts of my job is challenging the prejudices of people in the settled community, which can only be done well by my spending time with the Gypsies, Irish Travellers, New Travellers and Showpeople I meet, and then sharing some of their culture and struggles in my public presentations, radio interviews and conversations. Through sharing stories of accompanying Travellers with an often hostile audience there's the chance to dispel some of the myths constructed to separate. In my presentations I need also to be present with my audience and listen to their fear and anger because, if I don't, I know they'll never listen to me. It's all about building relationships.

BUILDING RELATIONSHIPS

I've learnt that being present on the ground and taking time to listen and understand a conflict are vital and sometimes lengthy first steps to build enough trust to begin to build up relationships between people in the midst of conflict. Like the conflict between Gypsies and Travellers and the settled population in the UK, the conflict around the border between the Karamajong people and the Iteso in north-east Uganda was one as old as time: between the Karamajong, who were nomadic pastoralists, and the Iteso, who were settled farmers.

Okolonya base was next to a road which marked the border, and mixed settlements of people from both tribes had begun to spring up all along it in response to and replicating the CHIPS base. The land was fertile and had reverted to overgrown bush during the 20 or so years of conflict, when it had been a kind of no man's land. With the brutal suppression of most of the cattle raiders by the Ugandan army and following CHIPS example, people were daring to return to the land and beginning to plant again and build houses.

I worked with Pusi and Luka, two former Karamajong warriors and cattle raiders, who were now members of the CHIPS peacekeeping team, building a house for Pusi, his wife and three children. First, we cast the bricks, digging up the red clay soil, mixing it with dung, dry grass and water, then adding the mixture to a mould, then once part dry, tapping it out to cook in the sun. Once the bricks were dry, we mixed up a mud mortar and built a round enclosure with a gap for a small door about six feet tall. Then with machetes, we hacked our way into the bush and cut about 20 four-inch round Y-poles, which we then surrounded the house wall with. Then we cut more long poles for the round roof, which we lashed together with thick leathery dried reed from a river bank. Then we summoned a dozen neighbours, raised the roof frame and placed it on the Y-frames around the wall, thus creating a roof with a small veranda all around the hut. Next, we cut dry grass and tied it in bunches, then we thatched the roof, using the reed to bind it to the roof frame. In a week we had built a house from nothing but local materials: not a nail or screw, piece of plastic, glass or any foreign body had been used, and when it had served its purpose, it would simply return to the ground from which it had come.

In the building of the house, through the gift of manual labour, I had befriended Pusi and Luka. I'd heard that in the Karamajong language there was no word for stranger and the next nearest word was enemy, that it took time to develop friendship with Karamajong people, but when you did, it was for life. By the end of the building of the house, we were fast friends. Out in Uganda, I was never in control. I was so new to living in the bush that I had to depend on the local team for everything, and I learnt that my safety depended on me building good, strong relationships with the local people. The better I accompanied them, the happier and safer I would be. That's how it was with Pusi and Luka once I'd built that house with them and established their friendship; I knew they would seek to protect me, and I began to let go of a lot of my fears.

Building relationships takes time, particularly with those who have different understandings of our world, and, sadly, many people in our busy world choose not to give or risk this time, preferring rather to stay enclosed in their circle of friends. Working with Travellers has taught me that it's always worth the extra effort and time to build trust. There's one site I visit in Salisbury which I hated visiting, as all I ever got from the people was a cursory nod as I walked round the trailers feeling useless and isolated. I persisted in going, and finally on the fourth visit someone decided to talk to me, and on the fifth visit I was offered tea. Now I know nearly all of them and have built friendships with a number, all the more precious and gratifying because I've had to work for it and build it.

One of my concerns before going out to the West Bank was who my housemates would be because I'd be spending three months sharing a small house with them, and I knew, through my experience of living in community, this could lead to much potential conflict. The first week our team was together we worked hard to get to know each other, particularly listening to what caused us stress. Ida said she got stressed when she was hungry, David when he was short on sleep, Sophie when she missed her friends and I said being indoors too much. We divided tasks in the house: I did most of the cooking, David the washing-up (he used to boast that we had a dishwasher in our house 'made in Taiwan'), Ida did all the computer work and stats, and Sophie took the lead in hosting visitors. We committed to eating together at least once a day, talking through any tensions between us and, consequently, were a very happy household. This was in marked contrast to other small teams in the programme, where there were often simmering tensions, which were of course heightened by the stress of living in a place occupied by a very proactive military. I stayed one night at the EAPPI house in Hebron and was told there was food in the fridge if I wanted anything or to go out and buy myself food.

That evening, the four people in that team sat in the same room but all operated as individuals, staring into their laptops, eating their own food. I eventually sent an email to one of them asking if she'd like a cup of tea! They were being typical Westerners, bringing to their team the individualistic mind-set of so many of us.

As peacemakers, I felt strongly that we had to live in peace with one another to cope with the conflict we were experiencing all around us, and to model a more relational way of being together. We were helped in this by the immense hospitality we experienced from people of the village, who lavished us with Palestinian hospitality. 'Ahlan Wha Salan!' people kept saying to us as we walked past their doors, which I knew meant welcome, but soon came to understand meant much more than welcome to the village. Rather it was 'Come into our homes and feel really welcome, sit with us, drink tea, drink more tea and eat with us.' I particularly enjoyed sitting outside people's homes, drinking tea in the late afternoon. As the winter light faded, a small metal brazier would be lit and fed with dried prunings from the village olive trees. There around the fire, people would tell stories of their families, talk about food, their hopes and fears, but all of it overshadowed by the difficulties of living under occupation. I loved the deeply relational nature of the Palestinians I met in the village, their sense of being part of the land they lived in, and the willingness they had to make time for each other. My mentor Graham Chadwick's words echoed in my mind: 'no word in Sotho for wasting time, only making time'. In contrast, when I visited an Israeli house on a settlement or in Israel, things were much more business-like, more Western middle class. You'd arrange a time to visit and be quickly asked what you wanted in a much more direct and functional way. Israel felt familiarly European and much more individualistic, whilst the West Bank felt more Oriental and community orientated. It seemed no wonder the two peoples were in conflict. Many of the Palestinians I met had a gift for accompaniment and were prepared to invest time in building relationships with others, and this gave me a sense of hope that the conflict could one day be resolved if people from both sides could safely meet one another.

The communality of Palestinian culture and its innate sense of hospitality seemed to mirror what I'd been striving to live out at Pilsdon. At Pilsdon, we sought to offer radical hospitality to whoever called; we were very good at it, and it came out of a very good ideological intention, but the hospitality I received from the Palestinian villagers felt like it came straight from the heart and was utterly natural. It convinced me that peace could happen in the region, so strong was this desire and commitment to welcome the stranger. Our landlord and head of the largest family in the village, Abu Assam, typified their welcoming nature. His hospitality was lavish and, after visiting his house a couple of times, I soon learnt to eat slowly, pace myself and leave my plate half full, otherwise it would be swiftly mounded up again. In spite of this, we never left his house without feeling we'd eaten too much, and always laden with bags of seasonal food, be it oranges, avocadoes or tomatoes, and it was always a struggle, sated and weighed down, to walk the half-mile uphill back to our house.

Abu Assam was a born peacemaker, a handsome and powerfully built man in his late fifties, with a jutting jaw, big expressive eyes, an assertive presence, and huge charm. He taught by telling stories. He had become politically active as a student in Cairo and had ended up in prison for protesting against human rights abuses in Egypt. He had always espoused non-violent resistance as the way to bring about peace and had been one of the founders of the 'Stop the Wall' group and the Land Coalition, which sought to challenge the legitimacy of the occupation and the building of the separation barrier. With great pride he told us how he had managed to win some of his land back, which had been taken to expand the adjacent settlement of Zufin, in the Israeli courts. It had been at a price though, his wife had been forced to sell all her jewellery to fund the legal expense. He used humour a lot to make a point and quoted Shelley and Shakespeare to back up his arguments. He insisted peace would only come through Israelis and Palestinians sitting down and talking to each other.

One evening, Abu Assam visited us at the house, and he seemed strangely subdued. I asked him what was wrong. He said he had a difficult meeting to go to the next day and would tell me about it once it was completed. The following evening he called in again, back to his ebullient best and told me what had happened. One of his sons was in prison for supposedly supporting Hamas, and another son, who was a building contractor, was in danger of going to prison. A man had died by walking into an empty lift shaft and falling six floors, on a building site this son was managing. As soon as news of this tragedy had reached him, Abu Assam had gone with other senior members of his family and visited the family of the deceased man to give condolences and had given a lump sum of 3500 Jordanian dinars (equivalent to £3500) as a goodwill payment to help with funeral costs. Many of Abu Assam's family had attended the funeral in the neighbouring village. Then, a week later, he had invited 300 guests from the dead man's family and people from his village to a large meal at the family home. A week after that, the meeting he was so apprehensive about had happened, with a few elders from each family and village discussing the accident and who was responsible, compensation, and so on. At the end of the meeting, the man's family decided that no one was to blame but the man himself, and it had been a terrible accident. The man's family then went on to thank Abu Assam for the support given them, and gave thanks that strong bonds of trust had now grown between both families and both villages. They also returned the £3500 Jordanian dinars and prayed that friendship and peace would continue to grow between both families.

This story illustrated for me the strongly relational nature of Palestinian culture, the commitment to listen to one another, take time to get to know each other's extended families, sit, eat, share time together, then reach a corporate conclusion. In terms of a way of making peace and building trust, it was hugely impressive. If this way of working together to build relationships was adopted and multiplied across the Israeli–Palestinian conflict as a whole, it would do much to dismantle the fixed and polarised positions people entrench themselves in, on both sides of the physical and psychological wall. When you take time to listen to the other, to be with them and share food with them, it becomes difficult to see them as the enemy any more. Of course, to be bold enough to sit down and eat with your enemy demands courage and the willingness to risk things going wrong and the condemnation of others.

RISK

In Northern Ireland, following the 1997 Good Friday Agreement, it was surprising for many to see how over the years, Ian Paisley, the staunchest and one of the most bigoted defenders of the union with Great Britain, became good friends with Martin McGuiness, a former military commander of the IRA, a friendship which led to them becoming known as 'the Chuckle Brothers'. Through spending time together and committing to peace, huge and ancient enmities had been broken down. Peace doesn't come about through the public theatre of signing peace treaties but through the slow and painstaking work of building up relationships and daring to risk extending the hand of friendship to those we have been taught are on the other side. This slow building of trust is well illustrated in the poem 'Shaking Hands' written by Padraig Ó Tuama, leader of the Corrymeela Community, a community dedicated to building peace in Northern Ireland. It is inspired by the Queen shaking hands with Martin McGuinness in 2012.

> *Because what's the alternative?*
> *Because of courage,*
> *Because of loved ones lost*
> *Because no more.*
> *Because it's a small thing shaking hands; it happens every day.*
> *Because I heard of a man whose hands haven't stopped shaking*
> *   since a market day in Omagh.*
> *Because it takes a second to say hate, but it takes much longer to*
> *   be a great leader,*
> *Much, much longer.*

Ó Tuama (2013, p.15)

Padraig Ó Tuama says that for any peacemaking process to begin, someone has to dare to go first. Risk extending the hand of friendship, knowing it may be rejected.

The week before I left Uganda, Luka wanted to give me something to take home, so took me honey collecting in the bush with Pusi. We found a hollowed-out old termite mound that had become a hive and, as the bees floated in and out, we collected a large fan of dried grass, lit it and began to smoke them out. I'd done a similar thing in the UK, the principle being that the bees under threat from the smoke feed on honey, and sated by it, become placid; but unlike in the UK, we had no protective suits or veils. Pusi lifted his T-shirt over his head, exposing his torso, as he prepared to put his hand into the hive.

'Why are you doing that?' I laughed.

'Oh, he hates getting stung on the head,' Luka replied.

Pusi reached into the hive and pulled out a chunk of honeycomb, as did Luka, then I copied them, shoving my unprotected arm in and triumphantly raising up a wad of dripping honeycomb, shaking any remaining honey-addled bees off it. Most of the comb went into a plastic bag for processing, but some got eaten right there; we filled our mouths full of honeycomb, munching it all, wax and grubs, honey oozing into our smiling mouths. I've never tasted anything so sweet and happy before. Later, around the evening fire, there was much laughter and when I asked for translation, they said they were laughing at the story of the crazy Mzungo who had put his hand into the beehive.

There's something about our willingness to take risks that is essential to peacemaking and moving relationships on. If we always play safe and stay in our own well-protected silos, life may well appear to be easier, but it's unlikely that our relationships with others will ever deepen. By risking naming the issue that's coming between us, there's the chance that conflicts and differences can be overcome. If we don't, then we'll never know whether change is possible, and things will just stay the same or get worse. When F. W. De Klerk, in South Africa in 1986, risked visiting Nelson Mandela in prison, it began the transformation of that deeply segregated country. By daring to cross the imagined borders between us, dialogue and the breaking down of the myth that conflict is inevitable become possible. Peace is not the absence of conflict but rather learning to live with it, understand it and seek to transform it. Real peacemaking is something that grows long term and you don't always see the fruit of your endeavours, but, in a small way, the growth of my friendship with Pusi and Luka was all part of the slow, long-term building of trust that makes peace possible and life so enriching. Accompaniment, if it is to be part of any peacemaking process, needs to metaphorically risk putting your hand in a beehive, to reach out to others we find different or difficult, or whom we fear, and offer to walk awhile with them the better for us to understand and grow in respect.

Living in community at Pilsdon had taught me that peacemaking wasn't something you left to the United Nations in some far-flung land but began in the difficulties of day-to-day relationships, and was something that demanded hard work and attention. We lived so much on top of each other at Pilsdon, sharing meals, work and common space, that if you fell out with someone, you'd never be able to avoid them; instead you'd be having to walk past them maybe 20 times a day. In the workplace, it's often possible to avoid people you don't like or are at odds with, and after work you get respite from any conflicts by going home, but living in community, the person was close at hand. I learnt, over time, that this was a blessing far more than a curse. Too often in Western society we are able to write off people we don't like: those who are different or whose personality or way of life challenges us. The often segregated and compartmentalised lives people increasingly live mean that distance from those we find uncomfortable to be around is easy to maintain. Work is increasingly individualised, increasingly dependent on technology, be it the person sitting at their computer all day or the farmer isolated in his state-of-the-art tractor. Even in the public sector, management has become so obsessed with outcomes that recording what you've done can take as long as actually doing it, which creates a lot of stress and tends to turn people inwards and looking at their individual performance rather than feeling part of a team. It's much easier to turn back to the screen and answer emails than it is to make time for and risk that difficult conversation that might resolve conflict and build relationships.

At Pilsdon, because of the proximity in which we lived, unresolved conflicts became almost intolerable, so I gradually learnt that it was better to face up to and deal with them. My natural instinct has always been to avoid conflict, but one thing living in community has taught me is that it's nearly always better to deal with things early rather than let things fester and grow. William Blake darkly describes how resentment can grow in his poem 'A Poison Tree':

> I was angry with my friend
> I told my wrath, my wrath did end
> I was angry with my foe
> I told it not, my wrath did grow.

Blake (1972, p.218)

The poem goes on to describe his foe lying dead under the poison tree he has created through the nurturing of toxic resentment. I learnt a lot from a number of people in recovery at Pilsdon, who taught me the dangers of what they call in Alcoholics Anonymous 'stinking thinking', which I understand to be the harbouring of resentments, which can turn into a negative cycle of thoughts against self and others. I always found it moving when people spoke honestly with me after I'd upset them or they'd got angry with me, telling me why I'd upset them, or were able to apologise with insight into an overly aggressive reaction to something I'd said or done. Much more difficult and energy sapping were the people who harboured and nursed their grievances, fuelling an unspoken but silently communicated anger. I tried not to be like that and, if someone upset me, I took the risk of dealing with the person directly, maybe not always immediately, as sometimes I needed to step back and process what was going on within me. Was I just really tired and looking to dump my frustrations on someone I found difficult? Was the person who upset me triggering some of my old unresolved fears and vulnerabilities? Was I just projecting my anger about something else onto them? The more extreme my reaction and anger, the more likely, I learnt, that it was due to some unresolved conflict in me. All this hard work of being prepared to stay with our difficult feelings towards others and be honest about our own woundedness demands a strong commitment and determination which is summed up for me in the Palestinian word 'Sumud'.

SUMUD

The day before we left the village of Jayous, we went to a 'Land Day' demonstration, which marks the day in 1976 when the Israeli government began to expropriate land from Palestinian farmers for state purposes. After three months of seeing the crushing realities of the occupation and pondering this day, which historically marked a further escalation in the conflict, I was feeling how small our contribution to peace had been against the weight of history, and sad about leaving friends in the village. Huge Palestinian flags waved defiantly, and raucous speeches seemed to sum up the polarised and entrenched nature of the conflict, and I felt dispirited. Then, a large smiling moustachioed Palestinian man came over, who I'd not met before, and thanked us for being in the village and sharing their life. 'Your pens and the stories you will tell will be more powerful than all the guns and bombs of the Israeli army.' These were the words I needed to hear, and as we crossed the border back into Israel, I suddenly felt a sense of hope, not despair. I'd gone to try and be part of bringing about change but what had really begun to change was something in me: I was leaving with a sense of hope, partly because of some of the very impressive and courageous Israeli peacemakers I had met and the incredible resilience of the Palestinian people summed up in the word 'Sumud', which means steadfastness and the ability to endure in spite of everything.

I had discovered this Sumud in myself, as I experienced some of the trauma that so many experienced and had struggled not to be crushed by it. I'd seen much that disturbed me, but the incident that I'd found most harrowing was the abuse of eight-year-old Emir by Israeli soldiers. I'd been staying in Hebron, probably the most conflicted city in the West Bank, where a group of some 500 fundamentalist Israeli settlers live next to the Tomb of the Patriarchs. They are protected by up to 2000 Israeli soldiers, who man 18 checkpoints in the centre of a city of 250,000 Palestinians. The day I was there, there was a riot involving Palestinian youth throwing stones at the army and the army returning fire with tear gas and sound bombs. Later in the evening, just as it was getting dark, I was out with Rachel, an Austrian Ecumenical Accompanier, in the town centre. We saw an army patrol go up the road in front of us, made up of a jeep followed by several armed soldiers. Experience told me it was a snatch squad, and they were looking to pick someone up. Just at that moment, Emir and his teenage brother were walking down the street about 50 yards from us. The jeep halted and two soldiers stopped the brothers, then they separated them. I watched in disbelief as they forced eight-year-old Emir into the back of the armoured jeep. Rachel captured the moment with her zoom lens, which showed the fear on the little boy's face, that look that I recognised from my own children just before they burst into tears. I ran up to the soldier who'd put him in the jeep to remonstrate with him, holding my hand three feet above the ground to demonstrate how small the child was. I knew he wouldn't, couldn't back down at that point, as a crowd had begun to gather in the street – he couldn't show what would be perceived as weakness and release the little boy. If I'd only got there a few seconds earlier and put myself between the jeep and the boy, a crowd would probably have gathered round and we might have saved him.

Instead, Emir was handcuffed and blindfolded in the back of the van, taken back to the barracks and left outside in a courtyard, still blindfolded and bound with a panting Alsatian dog next to him and settler children taunting him through the railings. He wet himself and was finally released back onto the streets at 11 p.m. to find his way home. My colleagues later visited the family and saw little Emir sitting white-faced in the corner. He'd hardly spoken since being picked up, and was having nightmares and wetting the bed. I was infuriated and filled with despair; what a brutal, humiliating thing to do, what better way to perpetuate hatred. I felt for the boy and his family, but I felt too for the soldiers being brutalised by the army's policy of arresting children and humiliating them. In May 2018, according to figures released by B'tselem, an Israeli human rights organisation, there were 291 Palestinian minors held in Israeli prisons, many no doubt traumatised like Emir by their experiences and filled with resentment against the occupation. What better way to perpetuate a conflict than by planting the seeds of hatred in the next generation?

A few days after this experience, I woke up crying in the night with tears of anger, despair and, most of all, guilt. I thought if only I had intervened earlier, I might have at least saved Emir. When I rationalised things and realised that he was one of 600–700 Palestinian children who go to prison each year, it didn't make me feel any better; I just felt the weight and enormity of the conflict. I didn't want to eat, I had difficulty sleeping, I felt dirty and ashamed, polluted by the toxicity of the conflict. I didn't know what to do. I'm usually pretty good at processing things, but I couldn't seem to work through this. I was beginning to feel overwhelmed. Then, early one evening just as it was getting dark, I went into my room, lit a candle in the corner and just sat and sat with my feelings and waited in silence. Just sitting there, listening to my breathing, not thinking, trying to do nothing. I felt drawn to do this for the next few nights, and slowly something began to shift in me. It was as though the act of lighting the candle was an act of resistance against the deep sense of evil I was experiencing, and by sitting with my despair, not running from it, not being crushed by it, I began to experience a deep sense of hope, and it was a hope that never left me. By learning to sit with or accompany my difficult feelings, somehow they lost their power to diminish me. Somehow, in confronting the harrowing darkness, I began to perceive a light beyond it and feel a strength to resist it. A hope that might feel fragile but was going to endure. Yes, I'd begun to understand and feel my own Sumud.

Of crucial importance to Roy Calvorcoressi, the founder of CHIPS, was a similar notion to Sumud, which he called 'bearing the enmity': the ability to keep going when everybody seems against you, and digging deep for the resources that will sustain you. For Roy, this was at the heart of peacemaking: to be prepared to live with a sense of fear and exclusion and somehow not to be crushed by it. He took as his model the crucified Jesus, who was prepared to take on the pain and projection of fear and anger from others, not respond with violence or protest but just stay with it, living in the hope that it would be eventually transformed. Peacemakers often find themselves stuck in the middle of a conflict, getting the blame from both sides, accused of favouring one or of being involved for their own financial benefit. Certainly, I felt the huge sense of enmity against our base at Okolonya from the neighbouring village, which had all been stirred up by a local politician telling a succession of lies about CHIPSs motivation for being there.

Several times in Uganda, CHIPS bases had their thatched roofs set on fire, and there had been a massacre at the Lomaratoit base in 2001, where three CHIPS workers had been killed, but rather than leave Uganda, the charity had decided to relocate elsewhere along the border. Eventually, more and more people began to settle around new CHIPS bases, and through the building of relationships with local politicians from both sides of the conflict, a sustainable peace was established. By 2010, over 40,000 people had resettled in mixed communities along the border, and old enmities were breaking down. Through daring to be steadfast in the midst of violence, by continuing to accompany people and build mixed settlements, CHIPS had played a significant role in dismantling a dangerous and deadly conflict.

What I'd learnt from community life, from my time in Israel/Palestine and working with CHIPS, was that the building of good relationships was at the heart of all peacemaking, and that to learn to be a peacemaker, I needed to learn humility and not be afraid of examining my own weaknesses, prejudices and vulnerabilities. The commitment to live peaceably also, I'm learning, takes time and effort, and it's easy to see why people choose the path of conflict, which is so much simpler to understand and define. In many ways, it's more comfortable to be polarised from somebody you dislike or think you hate than to do the work of listening to them and yourself in order to solve the conflict. It's easier to retreat behind a wall than risk living with discomfort, fear and uncertainty. In the maintenance work I did at Pilsdon, I noticed how I and others used to love doing demolition work, which was quick and simple and gave instant satisfaction. In contrast, people were more reluctant to join in the more complex and time-consuming task of building something, but when they engaged in the building process and completed something, it gave a lasting sense of pleasure and also much learning went on. Peacemaking through accompaniment is something that is built relationship by relationship, is fragile, demanding, sometimes full of conflict, never fully achieved, but I've noticed that when I'm seeking to walk in the way of peace with others, I experience a deep and lasting sense of joy.

I want to turn now to the most violent conflict in today's world. A conflict we too long have ignored and are still in deep denial about. A conflict that has been escalating without check over the past century, leading to the death of tens of thousands of people every year and the eradication of thousands of species and whole ecosystems: the ecocide we have been pursuing with increasing ferocity since we named it 'global warming' in the 1970s. If peace comes about through the building and rebuilding of relationships and learning how to belong together, of being with the other and risking crossing the walls we have erected around ourselves, then it's of vital importance that we rebuild our shattered relationship with Mother Earth. If being at peace is compared to feeling at home with others and ourselves, then it's of overwhelming importance that we learn to live well on the earth, our common home.

My journey of seeking to learn to accompany others will now begin to cover the ground of how to learn to be in a healthy, non-exploitative and fulfilling relationship with the myriad forms of life that surround us.

7

LIVING IN RELATIONSHIP WITH OUR PLANET

We're driving deeper into the hinterland of the hospital, past accident and emergency, past medical deliveries, when we spot the discreet sign 'Loading and Unloading for Hospital Morgue.' Brother Hugh backs the hire van into a screened-off area, and Brother Clark and I ring the intercom. We're all a bit nervous and knowingly use humour to disguise our unease. None of us has ever picked up a body before. We've all experienced the morgue vicariously through watching TV crime dramas, but this is real. We're here to pick up the mortal remains of Brother Giles, transfer him into a willow coffin, and take him back to the friary to remain overnight before his funeral.

We're let in by a fit-looking young man and do the paperwork, then a drawer is opened and a corpse covered in plastic is pulled out. The head is unzipped and Giles' grizzled and rather grey face is revealed.

'Do you want the plastic left on him?' the attended asks, looking at my rather amateurish coffin.

'No, let's take it off,' I reply. 'Don't worry, the coffin's lined with some breathable membrane I had left over from a roofing job, so it won't leak.' We definitely don't want plastic in our burial ground.

I cut away the plastic shroud and we tenderly lower Giles into the coffin, lined with wool from our sheep and a sheet from the

Hilfield laundry. We take one last look, say a prayer and another goodbye, and then tie down the wicker lid. Then we ease him out into the back of the van and we drive back to the friary.

Giles lies in the chapel overnight, and many come to sit and pray round the coffin through the night and early in the morning. We make the final preparations in our burial ground, checking the length, width and depth of the grave and the lorry straps that we'll use to lower him down. Half a dozen or so people have dug the grave, mainly young volunteers he'd been so kind to over the years, and it's their way of giving something back to him. In the morning it's busy in the kitchen, as people prepare the funeral feast, all made of home-grown meat, vegetables and salad. As people arrive, they're welcomed with tea and then the funeral Mass takes place. Giles' nephews, who are all burly farmers, carry him down to the graveyard as the big bell tolls out his 84 years. He's lowered into the ground, and many join in the filling of his grave. Then it's back to the courtyard where homemade wine and cordial from our elderflowers are served, followed by the food.

It's a fitting send-off for Giles, who'd been living a very full and giving life up to two weeks before he died, but also a tribute to the way Hilfield Friary seeks to honour both people and the planet, which is our common home. Giles was a great lover of nature, and it was a revelation to walk the short 20-minute 'triangle' walk with him in early spring, when he'd point out toothwort, star of Bethlehem, wood anemones and countless other wild flowers on the banks. His knowledge was good but more impressive was his delight in the beauty and wonder of it all. He used to say that one of the reasons he wanted to return to Hilfield to spend the last years of his life was because he was suffering from 'nature deficit disorder' living in London. In giving him a homemade funeral, we'd completely cut out the funeral directors, partly to save money, but more importantly to give Giles a more personal and environmentally friendly burial. As a Franciscan brother, he would have been well aware of St Francis' description of 'Sister Death' as something to be welcomed and natural, unlike the taboo that death has too often become in developed countries, where we pay others to handle the body, embalm it with formaldehyde, transport it, carry it, bury it or burn it for us. We've objectified death in our society and at Hilfield we try to reverse that process and see it as part of life.

In the same way, we have objectified nature, and I think the root of this malaise is our fear of the unknown, fear of our mortality, desire to be in control of our individual destinies, fear of wildness, so we have chosen isolation and insulation from nature rather than relationship with it. This objectification of nature has led to untold damage to our planet, but much of this could be reversed if we learn how to reconnect with it, re-enchant our relationship with nature, and recognise our addictive patterns and the tendency of twenty-first-century people to compartmentalise life. By learning to walk with and see ourselves intimately connected to the soil, the plants, the water, the air, the creatures that surround us and give us life, a more joyful and sustainable future is possible. Put simply, we need to relearn how to be with nature, how to accompany it and be accompanied by it.

For the first 35 years of my life, before I moved to rural Dorset, I lived a very urban existence largely cut off from nature in my daily life, always living in cities, focused on people but with little thought for the planet. That's how most of us today live; throughout the world, there are now, for the first time in human history, more people living in cities than in rural areas. In the UK, only 1 per cent of the population work directly on the land. Even in the UK, there is a relentless movement of the young from rural parts to the city, partly caused by the lack of jobs, lack of excitement, and the rising cost of housing caused by retirees moving to the countryside. For many of these urban 'incomers', their view of the countryside is as something that is quiet, withdrawn, peaceful, a good investment and not a living, breathing reality. Most farmers have a deep love and powerful emotional investment in their land, but economics and the drive for higher production and cheap food has meant that the farming industry has been systematically trashing the countryside and killing and eroding species upon species for the past 50 years.

It's estimated that agriculture contributes up to 23 per cent of greenhouse gases. If our farmers, who love their land, are unable to see the damage they are doing to our planet, what hope is there for the rest of us? Yet, I believe there is hope and it lies in re-enchanting our vision of the natural world and rebuilding our relationship with it, realising our dependence on what Brother Giles and Pagan friends call Mother Earth.

RE-ENCHANTING OUR RELATIONSHIP WITH THE EARTH

I never really gave much of a thought to nature. It was only when I went on holiday, usually somewhere near the coast or somewhere rural, or on days off walking with friends, that I chose and felt to be part of something bigger than my urban environment, and I noticed how I always felt restored and enlivened by it. I did also always dig up my garden and grow vegetables, and once had an allotment on a city farm in Liverpool, so the urge was there.

In 1996, I moved to rural Dorset, attracted not by the landscape but the chance to live in a community, living a life of prayer, manual work and the welcome of people in need. I'd probably have preferred an urban community, but Pilsdon was what was on offer. Slowly, my world view began to change, and I became enchanted with the physical place as much as the idea and reality of living in community.

Walking across a starlit field at 6 a.m. on a winter's morning, calling the cows in for milking, hearing the sound of the chain rattling on a gate breaking the deep silence, listening to the rumbling of the cow's rumen as I pressed close for warmth, and warming my hands on the udders as they squirted milk into a foaming stainless steel bucket was a magical way to start the day. After breakfast and the inevitable community meeting, I'd be out in the vegetable garden, on a wet day forking round the edges and shaking couch grass and bindweed free of the thick dark clay soil. If it was dry, I'd be double digging sections or shifting well-rotted manure onto a bed for the worms and rain to pull down nutrients into the soil. If it was really wet, we might climb into the minibus, drive down to the coast and collect seaweed for next year's tomatoes and today's compost heap, buffeted by the wind, all sound drowned out by the sea breaking on the shingle. Slowly, I was learning to be part of the landscape and, as the years passed, I seemed to identify as much with the hills, the trees and the plants as with the people there.

At Pilsdon, it was the cows who set the pace. The day began with milking at 6 a.m.; by 6.30 a.m. they'd be lumbering back into the fields and someone would be carrying the pails of milk down to the dairy to begin the process of filtering, pasteurisation and separating the thick Jersey cream. Milk jugs would then be carried into the dining room, ready for breakfast as the community slowly began to stir. Someone would come and sit on a bench outside for the first cigarette of the day, another would join them in a hushed conversation, and the day slowly began to take shape. The chapel bell would ring for morning prayer, and one or two would slowly gather in the chapel for worship. Looking back, I'm convinced it was the cows with their slow shambling gait and gentleness, as much as the remote setting and the simple prayers that were said in the church, that contributed to the peaceful atmosphere of the place. At 5 p.m. it was time for the second milking of the day, when you'd be more likely to have people chatting to you over the wall of the milking parlour and more background noise. What always amazed me about the afternoon milking was that you could start off milking feeling stressed by the events of the day, but as you emerged half an hour later from underneath a couple of cows all that stress seemed to have magically dissipated.

For some people, this rural idyll was too much. We had a young man come to stay with us from Bermondsey in South London and he was totally spooked by the silence and open space. He felt completely lost and unsafe in all the space. 'Where's all the buildings and buses?' he asked and, within an hour of arriving, we'd had to put him back on the train for London. At Hilfield Friary people coming for the first time from a city can be unsettled by the silence and threatened by the idea of making a retreat, slowing down, having no phone signal and super-slow broadband. I encourage them to listen to the wind in the trees, the flow of water, touch the moss in the woodland, smell the flowers, watch the flight of the birds and realise that out in nature there's just as much going on as in a city, but the rhythms are natural and feel life-giving.

At Hilfield, we try to promote this sense of enchantment and kinship with the immediate environment by providing seasonal guided walks, gently encouraging people to look, pay attention and feel part of the beauty around them. Brother Sam would take such delight in the arrival of the first swallows or on hearing a cuckoo that his enthusiasm spilled over boundlessly to all he communicated his joy and sense of wonder with. In this, he was following the example of St Francis, as Pope Francis has written:

> He was a mystic and a pilgrim who lived in simplicity and wonderful harmony with God, with others, with nature and with himself. He shows us just how inseparable the bond is between concern for nature, justice for the poor, commitment to society and interior peace. Francis shows us that an integrated theology takes us into the heart of what it is to be human. (Francis 2015)

This recapturing of the great joy and goodness at the heart of the natural world is the antidote to the cynical, blind and fearful pursuit of material wealth and growth at the heart of unregulated global capitalism. People aren't going to be persuaded to have less by listing the species that have died, dire warnings of rising sea levels and world hunger or by prophets of doom, even though all the science and facts point to this. Naomi Klein (2017, p.31), in her book *No Is Not Enough*, makes the argument for the need to provide a powerful new positive narrative to counter the dangerous and destructive path the world is on: 'The firmest of no's has to be accompanied by a bold and forward-looking yes – a plan for the future that is credible and captivating enough, that a great many people will fight to see it realised no matter the shocks and scare tactics thrown their way.'

Through offering courses on ecology and spirituality, days exploring our wildflower meadows, moth-catching evenings and butterfly days, along with living a simple, integrated and more sustainable life, Hilfield Friary seeks to be part of this positive narrative. By allowing people to see a positive and, crucially, joyful alternative through a gentle engagement with the land and world around us, we hope to encourage people to feel a growing sense of belonging to the earth, our common home. If society could fall in love again with the beauty and joy inherent in the natural world, there'd be huge motivation for rebuilding our fractured relationship with the earth. Out of this can come the motivation and the vision to confront the catastrophe that has been engulfing and eliminating myriad forms of life and surely awaits us in our so far protected existence and place of denial. Learning the joy of being with could be what saves us. For Michael McArthy (2015, p.246), it's the recapturing of this joy that will help save the planet, as he writes at the end of *Moth Snowstorm*:

> It will be a love which is informed, but it will also be a love, which recognising the scale of the threat, is engaged, a love which in delighting in a flower or a bird or a meadow or a marsh, or a lake or a forest, realises it may not be there next year and it will do whatever it can to protect it; a love which can be fierce.

Re-enchantment will motivate our desire to protect our planet but to bring about change, we will also need to ask why we have become so addicted to fossil fuels and a life of over-consumption and economics based on models of continuous growth in a world of finite resources. We'd need a world six times as large as this one if everyone in the world consumed resources at the rate of the USA. This model of unsustainable growth, frighteningly, is being pursued by the majority of respectable economic foundations. Why are we addicted to a way of life that is not sustainable and clearly so bad for us? One of the answers lies in our need to face up to these addictions and find healthy ways of relating to our world.

WILD HUNGER

In his book *Wild Hunger* (1998), Australian philosopher Bruce Wilshire argues that our Western lifestyle is deeply addictive and caused by a loss of what he calls 'ecstatic kinship' with the natural world. Not so many generations ago we were all hunters and gatherers and certainly it's only been in the past 150 years or so that the majority of people no longer work on the land. He argues that the loss of the natural highs and lows experienced when we were hunters and gatherers, and the loss of our ability to stimulate the natural opiates or endorphins produced to counteract pain, hunger and threat, has made us prey to addictive behaviour. So few people now work on the land, outdoors or with their hands that we have become cut off from these natural ways of helping us live with pain and loss. Instead, we seek other ways to make us feel better, which give us an unnatural high, but this doesn't last and fully satisfy us, so we want more, which leads to a cycle of addiction: 'Addictions try to fill the emptiness left by the loss of ecstatic kinship. They are substitute gratifications that cannot last for long – slavishly repeated attempts to keep the emptiness at bay. Finally, they drain the body of its regenerative powers' (Wilshire 1998, p.6).

I read this book when I was at Pilsdon living with a number of people in recovery from addiction, and it made immediate sense to me. One of the reasons Pilsdon seemed to work for people in recovery was precisely this unusual proximity to the land, the joy of being outside in all weathers, daily physical challenges and the healing power of animals. I've already mentioned the restorative powers of hauling wood from my friend Bill's neighbouring farm, but splitting wood in the farmyard at Pilsdon had great appeal to a number of men there.

There was a lovely soft-spoken Scottish West Highlander, Hugh, who loved splitting wood. He was a highly addictive person, who'd been seriously addicted to heroin. After he'd left the army he'd managed to come off it, but transferred his addiction from heroin to alcohol. He had a few goes living with us, usually coming in a poor state, living with us for several months, leaving apparently restored, falling off the wagon, then returning to us. We were always ready to have him back as he was an honourable person, completely honest about his need to address his addiction and strongly committed to community life. Once, when he returned to us, he was still coming off the drink and went into a psychotic episode. He disappeared for the night, only to dramatically return, chased into the farmyard by our neighbour Ian, who'd found him sleeping in his garage. He ran in with wild, terrified eyes, on bleeding bare feet, in a pair of boxer shorts and a torn T-shirt, scratched all over by brambles. He was the perfect image of 'wild hunger', an outer manifestation of the inner pain and disconnection that too often leads to addictive and self-destructive behaviour. I calmed Ian down and Hugh went to bed.

The next day, I asked if he wanted to see a doctor.

'You mean so I can have more drugs to get addicted to?' he replied. 'No. Give me an axe and a pile of wood and I'll start to feel better.'

Everyone seems to be addicted to something these days, be it sugar, coffee, shopping, gambling, pornography, seeking to fill some kind of apparent need. Then soon the only need becomes the need to have the thing we thought would make us feel better but now we crave for. What Hugh instinctively knew and I'm still learning is that the cravings we have never really satisfy, but what does help and can be healing is a real physical engagement with real natural things rather than following our greedy appetites. In the Tibetan Buddhist tradition, these things that we always want more of they call 'hungry ghosts'. Huge energy goes into feeding addictions and they can become so all-consuming that everything else is neglected. I wonder if, on a macro scale, we in the West have become so addicted to consumerism and technology that we have cut ourselves off from what really satisfies. The growth in people seeking allotments, and younger people seeking the natural highs of rock climbing, diving or other challenging sports speaks of a desire to satiate this wild hunger by connecting, through sport and the outdoors, with the highs and lows experienced by our hunter-gatherer ancestors.

The most lasting image I have of Hugh is not the distraught bedraggled fugitive but rather of him carrying a large lamb draped over both shoulders after he'd rescued it from a tangle of brambles in a hedge and carried it back to its mother ewe. At Pilsdon, work with the animals was key for a lot of people in helping them break the cycle of addiction. Being trusted to care for another living, breathing creature gave people a role in community life, a purposeful job, a sense of self-worth, but also helped them connect, or in Hugh's case reconnect, with the healing power of nature. The pigs were always particularly good at communicating with people and seemed the quickest to bond and build friendship with whoever was husbanding them – maybe because they didn't use words, words which are too often used to condemn, diminish and belittle people. Their needs were simple: twice daily feeding, checking their water, mucking out when they were indoors and lots of affection. Rubbing behind the ears, backscratching and tummy tickling all produced deep and noisy appreciation. Simple pleasures. They knew how to accompany people.

Julie Plumley runs a remarkable charity in Dorset called Future Roots, which began out of her frustrations of 20 years working as a social worker. No matter how hard she tried with her clients, many of whom suffered with addictions, she rarely managed to bring about any lasting change in their lives. She knew she couldn't go on much longer with this sense of disillusionment so decided to set up a charity working with children who had been or were about to be excluded from school, some of whom were living in the care of the local authority, to try and bring change to their lives before it was too late. Julie had grown up on a farm and knew the healing power of animals, so decided to buy a small farm and base her project around teaching and mentoring her young people using animals as the teachers too, in a non-institutional way.

The feel of the farm is remarkable. You walk into a muddy farmyard where young people are pushing wheelbarrows and mucking out the pigs, someone's opening a bale of straw and shaking it into the cows' winter quarters, there's a youngster learning to reverse a trailer behind the barn, a group of people with learning difficulties are on a walk, laughing at the ducks in the pond, chickens scurry out of your way. The classroom is entered via a porch where everyone leaves their wellies. There's always a high ratio of staff to pupils and lots of one-to-one work. The results are impressive.

At 13 C had been excluded from school. He wouldn't write, was aggressive and abusive. He was drinking and totally self-reliant with whatever money his mum left for him. His house was uncared for and definitely not a place of safety. His father was an alcoholic and abusive.

Social services, CAMHS and the police all failed to get him to open up and therefore did nothing.

He started to come to the farm – he was bright, valued the trust we put in him, our consistent boundaries and support. He was respectful and didn't swear. He never told us his full story but if our cows could talk... His confidence grew and although his home life deteriorated at times – he became homeless sometimes walking through the night to keep warm – he stuck with us, passed his first qualification here and then went on to an agricultural college where he passed several courses.

He is 18 now and doing brilliantly as an apprentice on one of the local farms, living at home again and has a better relationship with his mother. (Future Roots 2016)

Future Roots also now works with older people, many of whom are former farmers who, due to age or disability, have become socially isolated and vulnerable. Twice a week, a minibus picks people up from surrounding villages and farms and delivers them to the 'Countryman's Club', where they sit in an old barn, often on straw bales, and take part in some planned activities such as singing or craft work, or they help with the animals. I go in occasionally to do some basket making with them, but the most important thing is the companionship and having somewhere to belong. It's just not like your average institutional old peoples' club, it's literally down to earth, you can go and lean on a gate, listen to the chickens clucking, stroke a cow, hear young people arguing, and unlike in an old people's home you can see the sky.

I ask Julie if she thinks Future Roots would work in an urban setting. 'No, not in conventional classrooms or community rooms. Maybe on a city farm or something. But what makes here work, apart from the dedication of my staff and volunteers is all this.' She smiles, expansively opening her arms to indicate the farm. I completely understand; it's so obvious, really, that if we live as we were designed to do, in close proximity to the natural world, we are likely to be much happier and fulfilled. What's so impressive about Future Roots is the way the young people are mentored and accompanied both by Julie and her team but also by the animals on the farm.

Recent academic research backs this up and has coined the phrase beloved of Brother Giles, 'nature deficit disorder', to describe the negative effect of living in a world cut off from the healing power of nature. In a study of the effect of the proximity of green vegetation and hedgerows on people's mental wellbeing in an urban environment, Daniel Cox and others show how just seeing a bit of greenery each day can have a positive effect on people's health. The study concludes by saying in rather scientific language, 'This study shows that quantifiable reductions in the population prevalence of poor mental health can be achieved if minimal thresholds of vegetation cover are met' (Cox et al. 2017).

Studies into the onset of Alzheimer's disease have also shown reductions in its advance when people engage regularly in outdoor activity. I know from experience that just half an hour weeding in the vegetable garden is exactly what I need after a two-hour meeting stuck indoors. I feel my heart rate slow, my stress levels reduce.

Romany Gypsy Michael 'Duggie' Johnson is in total agreement about the benefits for all people subject to addiction, but particularly nomadic people, in spending time outdoors. He recently took me up Constitution Hill, overlooking Poole Harbour, and as we sat on the bench sipping tea, he showed me the place members of his family had camped 60 years ago before the major development of Poole which had led to the forced settlement of Gypsies in the area. Other favourite stopping places in the area named by the itinerant Gypsies, like Monkeys Hump Lane, Sugar Knob Mountain and, my favourite, Heavenly Bottom, have now all been built on, and the Gypsies who camped there moved into houses or the council-run site under electricity pylons and next to the town dump. For Michael and many other Travellers, forced to settle in houses, which they call 'bricks and mortar', always feels constraining and claustrophobic to those hard wired for the outdoor life. The old Gypsy wagons, or vardos, may have been small, but people generally lived most of the time outside, always cooking on an open fire, sitting out in whatever landscape they pulled up in. If you enter a traditional vardo, it always seems bigger than it is due to the positioning of mirrors to attract maximum light into the living space. Time and again, settled Travellers say they feel hemmed in living in 'dark houses' and forced into a sedentary lifestyle. This, in turn, affects people's mental health. If you're an Irish Traveller or Romany Gypsy, either settled or itinerant (which due to excessive enforcement policies brings additional stress), you're three times as likely to feel anxious and four times as likely to feel depressed as those in the general population (Parry *et al.* 2004, para.3.6).

Forced settlement of the nomadic people of this land can be compared to the plight of native people in North America, hemmed in on reservations, as also happened to the New Forest Gypsies, who were moved in the 1920s from their traditional stopping places in the forest into the notorious New Forest compounds to make way for an influx of urban campers into the newly established national park. The forced settlement of nomadic people all over the world seems to make them more vulnerable to addiction, as the loss of a healthy outdoor life is replaced by the sedentary life. There are high levels of addiction amongst the settled Gypsies of Poole, and this is something that Michael is determined to help combat. He openly talks to me and anyone who will listen about the ruinous effect of alcohol addiction on his life, leading him into crime and stretches in prison and psychiatric hospital. He's opened a remarkable fitness and non-contact boxing club in the local church hall, encouraging local Gypsies and others to use sport as a way of combating addiction. When I visit, there are always 40-plus people there: men, women, girls and boys, either fitness training or punching flexible rubber torsos, drops of sweat flying round the room, and others just sitting round, sipping tea, feeling part of something which gives the community a sense of fighting back. All the equipment is moveable so the club is nomadic, able to move from place to place, and training sessions sometimes happen on the beach. It's all about encouraging people to release those beneficial endorphins, giving them a natural high rather than resorting to alcohol and drugs. Michael is a keen walker, walking dozens of miles each week, like Satish Kumar and many before him, recognising the benefits of moving at a natural pace. He aims to take a group of young people walking and camping along the Dorset coastal path twice a year, with the support of the local lifeboat charity, to let them also experience the benefits of the wild outdoors, and put them in touch with their nomadic roots. It's not so long ago that we were all nomadic hunter-gatherers. Humans have only been settled for, at most, 500 generations, whilst we were hunter-gatherers for 50,000 generations before then. We could all probably do with a little more wildness.

In his poem, 'The Peace of Wild Things', farmer, poet and environmentalist Wendell Berry (1999, p.30) seems to capture this sense of the healing property of nature:

When despair for the world grows in me
And I wake in the night at the least sound
In fear of what my life and my children's lives may be
I go and lie down where the wood drake
rests in his beauty on the water and the great heron feeds
I come into the presence of wild things
Who do not tax their lives with forethought
Of grief. I come into the presence of still water.
And I feel above me the day-blind stars
Waiting with their light. For a time
I rest in the grace of the world, and am free.

It's these simple, natural pleasures that seem to be the best, life-saving and life enhancing, for, paradoxically, living with less seems to give us more, because with less we're more likely to learn to be with the natural world.

LEARNING TO LIVE WITH LESS

Hilfield Friary is a Franciscan community, seeking to follow in the way of St Francis, who rejected the wealth of his cloth merchant father to become an itinerant preacher, and embraced a life of voluntary poverty. Hilfield owns 45 acres of land and has eight buildings. I sometimes wonder what Francis would make of our material wealth. We try to adhere to his spirit and make it relevant for today by maintaining a life of prayer, seeking to live simply, welcoming people from all kinds of backgrounds and places, particularly those in need, and we have a particular emphasis on managing our land and daily life in an environmentally friendly manner.

Living simply means that we pay attention to what and how much we consume as a community. We now buy our electricity from Ecotricity, who only sell electricity from renewable resources, and generate some of our own from 40 solar panels on the chapel roof. We recently installed our own district heating system, which is a large biomass boiler burning woodchip, which we source from our own trees and council-owned land on the hill above us. Putting the system in meant digging over 300 metres of deep trenches for the pipework and drilling through the foundations of houses – real hard work, but it galvanised the whole community in a joint enterprise which was inspired by the vision of a world where we no longer burn fossil fuels. We've begun to wrap all our buildings in insulation to reduce the amount of energy we need to heat them, have installed solar thermal panels to heat water and are looking to build a new eco-house to encourage others to believe that green building is possible.

With transport, we encourage our visitors to come by train and heap praise on those who cycle to us. We also have an electric car which we use for the many short journeys we make. The community always plans our transport each day, so that we can fill cars up and cut out unnecessary journeys. Living in the country, ten miles from the nearest town, you can't just pop out for that extra pint of milk; if we run out of something, we wait for the next trip to town. I remember watching the community minibus return home in my first week at Pilsdon. Out of it came three people from the train station, six sacks of potatoes, ten four-metre lengths of timber and four carcasses of freshly slaughtered pigs. I knew then I'd quickly have to learn to multitask living in the country.

When we kill a pig at Hilfield, we try to honour the animal by using all of it. When we say goodbye at the very local abattoir, we always give the slaughter man a plastic pot to save the blood, which we use for making black pudding. When the pig comes back, we butcher it, using everything we can. Extra skin is used for pork scratchings or wrapping up other joints of meat, the trotters are boiled up for gelatine, the head is boiled for brawn, the heart, lungs and kidneys minced for faggots, bones boiled up for stock and excess fat used for making salami. We try to be true to the old saying that the only part of the pig you can't eat is the squeak. Though a vegetarian for 30 years, I join enthusiastically in processing the dead animals, as my vegetarianism doesn't particularly come from a reluctance to kill animals, but is motivated by the knowledge that present rates of meat consumption in the world are completely unsustainable. It seems mad that the wild grasslands of the Pampas in Argentina have been ploughed up to grow soya to produce grain-fed beef, when just a tenth part of that same soya would provide us with the same amount of protein as the beef.

At Hilfield, we're mindful of this and have an understanding that we only eat meat or fish three times a week. We try, too, to adhere to the LOAF principles: local food where possible, organic, animal friendly and fairly traded. Recently, in Lent, we decided to eat nothing that wasn't grown in the UK; this wasn't an extreme form of nationalism but an exercise to become aware of the distance food sometimes travels before it arrives on our plate. Meals were plainer – no spice, no rice, no pasta, no tinned tomatoes, all things regularly part of our diet – but we discovered new things like barley, groats and Marmite® pie. We do try and eat seasonally, using our own and locally grown vegetables, and out of season using fruit and veg frozen in a time of plenty. A lot of care and thought goes into the preparation of food for, as well as meal times being an expression of our common life (we all eat together), what we eat reflects our values.

In 1981, Carlo Petrini, an Italian wine critic, was so enraged by an application by McDonalds to open a fast food outlet on the Spanish Steps in Rome that he began the Slow Food movement in protest. It has, at its heart, the desire to promote local food, using local ingredients. Out of this grew the Citta Lente, the slow cities movement, what we would call Transition Towns in the UK. The principles of these worldwide movements include learning to live with less, and building more just and sustainable societies at a local level. As the UK Transition Town's website states, 'We respect resource limits and create resilience – The urgent need to reduce carbon dioxide emissions, greatly reduce our reliance on fossil fuels and make wise use of our precious resources is at the forefront of everything we do' (Transition Network 2016).

At Hilfield, we try and make wise decisions about what we consume. Just as we try to eat every bit of the pig, anything left over goes back in the fridge to return as soup on a Tuesday or Friday, or on a Monday, which is left-overs day. Anything we still haven't eaten and which has a possibility of poisoning someone goes into the council food recycling bin.

Recycling is also an important part of our life. We do all the plastic, paper and bottles stuff, but try too to recycle clothes, which end up as cloths; old boots become flower pots, unfixable furniture is dismantled for spare parts, old car tyres are used for a wormery. Out in the bush in Uganda, two hours from the nearest town, I was constantly amazed how people reused and made the very most of their resources. Old vegetable oil tins with 'USA FOOD AID' printed on them would be flattened and nailed on to the tiny wooden doors that kept the animals out of their huts to strengthen them. I watched someone cutting nails in half to make them go further, and old bicycle inner tubes would be used for tying things onto the backs of motorbikes. Bits of broken crockery would be used instead of sandpaper, to smooth the handles of handmade spoons. In rural Uganda you rarely saw litter, as people were living with so little and anything they had would be precious, used and reused. Young men would proudly wear a Manchester United football shirt, ten years old, that no youth in the West, where a new shirt is marketed by the club each year, would have been seen dead in. Clothes and shoes would be constantly repaired, restitched, resoled with car tyres or whatever was available. In the Solomon Islands the beaters for their pan pipes would be fashioned from recycled flip flops.

Whilst in the Pacific, I was shocked to hear that Cyclone Pam had destroyed over half the houses on the main island of Vanuatu, presumably leaving tens of thousands homeless. What I didn't realise was that nearly all those homes would have been constructed of local materials and could be rebuilt in a couple of days. Much more serious for the islanders would be the loss of that season's banana and coconut crops. In the Solomons, people would put up a house very quickly, and it would be constructed entirely of local materials: wood or bamboo for the house frame, coconut palm woven into the walls, and sago palm for the roof. The only furniture would be handwoven sleeping mats made from coconut palm and a set of metal cooking pots, which people would use on a wood-fuelled fire outside. The diet was locally sourced: fish from the sea, cassava, sweet potato or taro, another root crop, and local vegetables like slippery cabbage. I once went to a market between coastal and mountain people where no money changed hands. Instead, fish from the sea were bartered for root crops and tobacco from inland. Pigs or chickens would be killed for a special occasion, and the only imported food would be Solomon rice, rather misleadingly grown in New South Wales in Australia, or super noodles made in China.

When I ate with the team in Uganda, the food was always the same, with little flavour: always a single chapatti with black tea for breakfast, and 'posho' (a tasteless white mash of rehydrated sorghum and cassava flour) and beans for lunch and supper, with nothing in-between. When we ate, we were always hungry and deeply appreciative for what we had, and when there was an occasional variation, such as when someone found us an ostrich egg or killed a warthog, it felt like a feast indeed.

The simplicity of my life in Africa had a spare beauty and each day seemed packed with simple pleasures. The freshness of the early morning, the golden light of the first hour, the taste of the first cup of tea, the joy of hand pumping water at the borehole, the appreciation of the shade of a tree at midday, the sparing use of the litre of water to wash with before it got dark and the mosquitos came out, the fire to gather round to warm and light us on dark starlit nights. At Okolonya we were two hours on the back of a motorbike (if there was one available) from the nearest hospital so, where possible, we sought to use local medicine. We grew a plant, artemisia, which had strong anti-malarial qualities, used papaya sap and also the aloe vera plant for wounds, boiled papaya leaves for stomach disorders and used garlic and ginger to boost the immune system. We also drank lemongrass tea, which helps mitigate some of the fever that comes with malaria and other infections.

The biggest culture shock from living so simply in Uganda wasn't getting used to life with so little, but returning home and being confronted with excess and feeling overwhelmed by the constant choice. Paradoxically, I'd felt more at home in Africa and that, I think, is something to do with the joy that is invoked by simple living, and living in more immediate relationship with nature. It's simple pleasures that really satisfy. I'd learnt that living with less had given me far more. In Africa and the Solomons, I saw people living joyfully with a deep sense of gratitude for the little they had; in the UK, I saw people tense and miserable, complaining in their incomparable wealth. What was most noticeable to me was how people with less seemed to value and make more of their relationships with each other and their relationship with the natural world they were so closely connected to.

INTERCONNECTEDNESS

The first time I went swimming on the coral reef in the Solomons, I asked Brother Barto if there were sharks there. 'Yes sometimes', he said. 'But you don't need to worry, they are our friends.' Having grown up in the era of the film *Jaws*, I could never quite get the fear of sharks out of my mind, but I knew if I always swam with Brother Barto, friend of the sharks, that sense of relationship would keep me safe. Swimming out onto the reef was like going from watching a black-and-white film into glorious technicolour. There was such a profusion of life, of texture, of movement and colour it was a remarkable sensory feast. A coral reef is a complex ecosystem and, when in natural balance, capable of sustaining a vast number of species of fish, shellfish, invertebrates and plant life. The biggest threat to coral reefs, apart from bleaching caused by global warming, is the killing of sharks for shark fin soup. As a top predator, sharks maintain the balance of the ecosystem but when they are removed, too many other predators flourish and begin to destroy the whole ecosystem, particularly fish stocks. So Brother Barto was right in his rounded, relational understanding of the ocean: sharks are indeed our friends. The study of sharks or any ecosystem shows that we are all interconnected, and it's the loss of this wisdom and the tendency to objectify the natural world as something separate to us that has led to the ecocide human beings have been waging against the earth.

At Pilsdon, there was a man called Rupert, who'd been a deep sea fisherman and later on a tree surgeon, or arboriculturist as he liked to call himself. He came to us because he said he was drinking two bottles of vodka a day, which he didn't think was a very good idea whilst climbing trees. He managed to stop drinking and lived with us enthusiastically and well for a couple of years, doing some tree work and rejoicing in looking after the chickens, ducks and geese. Rupert had had a mystical experience whilst on watch at sea in the middle of the night and, as a result, had a deep sense of the interconnection of all things. He used to love quoting to me, by heart, part of William Blake's poem 'America' (1972, pp.198–199):

> Let the slave grinding at the mill run out into the field,
> Let him look up into the heavens and laugh in the bright air,
> Let the unchained soul, shut up in darkness and in sighing,
> Whose face has never seen a smile in thirty weary years,
> Rise and look out; his chains are loose, his dungeon doors are
>   open;

And let his wife and children return from the oppressor's scourge.
They look behind at every step and believe it is a dream,
Singing, the Sun has left his blackness and has found a fresher
    morning,
And the fair Moon rejoices in the clear and cloudless night,
For Empire is no more and now the Lion and Wolf shall cease,

For everything that lives is holy
For everything that lives is holy
For everything that lives is holy
For everything that lives is holy.

Rupert had as strong sense that everything and every creature that lived had a deep inherent value. His love and enthusiasm for trees conveyed itself to me. I'll never forget his delight at intoning, 'Fraxinus Excelsior! What a royal name for a royal tree, the ash tree, Fraxinus Excelsior, what splendour in the name that reflects the splendour of a fully grown ash.' He maintained that a tree had as equal a right to life as anyone else. One day I had to stop him assaulting Brian, a rather grumpy but kindly member of the community, for kicking one of Rupert's beloved geese. We barred him from the community for a week; he was repentant about lifting up and shaking Brian but not about his justifiable anger for protecting the goose who, in his eyes, was of equal value to anyone else.

Like John Muir, the nineteenth-century Scots/American, Rupert was a deep ecologist, seeing the inherent worth of all life regardless of its use to humans, and the need to live in relationship with all of nature. I know Rupert would have loved the story of John Muir tying himself to the top of a Douglas fir tree in a storm to experience the full force of nature as the tree would. The term 'deep ecology' was coined in 1972 by the Norwegian philosopher and mountaineer Arne Naess, who talked about the need for a deep ecological movement that began to question our fundamental values and relationship towards the natural world. This was in contrast with what he described as the shallow ecological movement, which was more concerned with finding technological fixes. These movements aren't, of course, incompatible and need to work in partnership but unless we change our fundamental human-centred world view, like Naess, John Muir and Rupert did, we're unlikely to bring about the deep-seated change to human behaviour which is so urgently needed. If this change comes from a place of love, respect and connection to all systems of life on our planet, then it can indeed bring the deep shift we need. Charles Eisenstein (2013, p.51) puts it well:

> We need to understand nature, the planet, the sun, the soil, the water, the mountains, the trees, and the air as sentient beings whose destiny is not separate from our own. As far as I know there's no indigenous person on earth would deny that a rock bears some kind of awareness or intelligence. Who are we to think differently?

Eisenstein says that until we stop objectifying nature and until we begin to see it as a living entity of which we are merely part, we'll continue on our path of destruction. If we never see forests as living beings rather than only a collection of trees, then there's no reason not to exploit them. The reason materialistic capitalism is killing so much of the world's life is because it sees it as already dead. If we begin to see nature as a living, breathing reality, we might realise how it has the power to a heal us and to heal itself.

Back in the early years of the thirteenth century, Francis of Assisi instinctively intuited all this and today is dubbed the Patron Saint of Ecology, because of his deep reverence for all forms of life. Living close to the earth, in simple lodgings and often sleeping out in the open, he was in tune with his environment. He had what Bruce Wilshire describes as a sense of ecstatic kinship with all creatures. He had a particular love of worms and birds, and is famously painted by Giotto preaching to the sparrows. His contemporary and biographer, Thomas Celano, writes of him, 'He was filled with compassion towards dumb animals, reptiles and other creatures. In the most extraordinary manner, never experienced by others, he discerned the hidden things of nature in his sensitive heart' (Armstrong, Hellmann and Short 1999, p.248). In 1224, towards the end of his life and nearly blind, Francis wrote the 'Canticle of the Creatures', a great song of praise in which he addresses Brother Sun, Sister Moon, Brother Fire, Sister Water and Mother Earth to illustrate his absolute sense of connection and fraternity/sorority with all things.

At Hilfield, we've created from a piece of waste ground what we call the Canticle Garden. Visitors can walk around it barefoot, experiencing Mother Earth beneath them. There is a sculpture of Brother Sun, a mosaic of Sister Moon and a wind sculpture of Brother Air; a fountain and stream pass through, and there are various sensory plants. The invitation is to connect with creation through making a sensory and prayerful walk through its elements.

Many people who come to stay at the friary ask us whether we're self-sufficient and we reply that we are not; partly because we couldn't grow enough food to support the many visitors we have, but also because we don't believe in the idea of doing and growing everything ourselves. We like to be in relationship with the water mill we buy our flour from, the organic farm we get our extra veg from, the wholefood merchant who sells us fairly traded dry goods. Rather than hiring a contractor, we'll ask a local farmer to dig out foundations for us or loan his mini-digger in return for goods in kind and only cash if really necessary. We know from our wildflower meadow, which supports eight kinds of orchids along with a multiplicity of species of grass and insects, that biodiversity and a web of complex relationships are what build resilience in a community. We recently managed to buy some more land, which we'll use partly for sheep and cattle and to grow wood for our heating system, but we also want to farm it in a way that allows the richest diversity of life possible to flourish. We're in partnership with the local council, Dorset Wildlife Trust, English Nature and four of our neighbouring farmers, all of whom have a vision of creating a species-rich habitat all along our shared land. We're hoping for the return of the Duke of Burgundy, not some long-lost French aristocrat, but rather a yellowy brown butterfly rarely seen in these parts and never on Friary land for over 40 years. It's a complex job to get everybody together to talk about having a shared management plan which will create favourable conditions for a species-rich grassland on the edges of woodland, but will be well worth it when we see the Duke return.

It's this commitment to work together, out of a love for and for the sake of a richer local environment, that I believe needs to be at the heart of ending the environmental catastrophe we are now in. Too often, even amongst activists for social change, there have been damaging splits. Commenting on the non-violent direct action taken by Extinction Rebellion on 17 November 2018, when 5000 people shut five London bridges, whilst at the same time in another part of London 30,000 people marched against fascism, Daniel Voskoboynik (2019) calls for a need for integrated, combined action against global injustice:

> This thinking of separations ironically runs counter to the nature of ecology, which is fundamentally concerned with the connections that sustain life. To put on the glasses of ecology is to see a world of intersections and interactions. It is to realize that common threads bind together environmental destruction, inequality, racial exclusion, poor health, violence, patriarchy and poverty.

What is it that will bring about the massive change in heart and harness political will to reverse years of complacency towards our planet and its poorest people? What will bring about the ending of the objectification of people and our planet and current polarising tendencies, and challenge unregulated global capitalism, isn't a new political movement, but rather what Jonathon Porritt, former director of Friends of the Earth, described as 'a spiritual revolution': 'What's needed in the current situation...is not so much a cap on carbon emissions, important though this may be, but a radical re-orientation of the way we see ourselves in relation to the natural world around us, something akin to a spiritual revolution' (Dubord 2016).

8

COMING HOME TO OURSELVES AND FINDING OURSELVES IN OTHERS

It's a beautiful August evening. The golden light reflects off the tail of the tiny plane as it taxies towards me. I check my parachute and tug nervously on the straps, I climb into the plane with three others and we begin our ascent. It takes 25 agonising minutes to get to the 11,000 feet we need to be at to make the jump. I've spent the past six weeks worrying about this jump, with a regularly repeated dream of falling, falling and then waking up just before I hit the ground filling my nights. As the plane judders upwards, I look at the man opposite me biting his nails; as I grin companionably at him, he returns me a sickly smile. I check my parachute again and know there's no turning back. Over 100 people have pledged money for the jump, fundraising for my son's rugby tour to China; I fear the shame of backing out of it even more than the anxiety of the jump. I face my fear, realising that I might die but it's highly unlikely, as the parachute is timed to open after 30 seconds and if it doesn't, all I need to do is pull the rip cord on the emergency back-up chute. I tell myself my life's been mostly very good up to now, and if it ends today, I've lived well and been given much, and for the next few minutes I distract myself with going over the highlights of my first 37 years on the planet.

Then it's time to go. I shuffle over towards the open door, sit on the edge, clinging to the shuddering sides of the plane, with my back to the abyss below me. I pause and all I can do is trust. Trust in my training, trust in the equipment and trust in God. Then I push off and let go, rolling backwards. At first, I have a sense of falling, but as soon as I'm in position, hands and legs stretched out, downward facing, it just feels like I'm floating. I can hear the air rushing past, but I have no sense of falling, just floating, totally free; it's remarkable, all my anxiety has fled and I feel utter joy. Then the parachute opens and there's a sensation of hard braking, and it feels like I'm going back up in the air; and then a few minutes of gentle descent watching the ground slowly come closer. Suddenly there's a tap on my back – in the exhilaration of the descent I've forgotten Dave, the Royal Marine, strapped to my back. 'There's no breeze to steer into as we land, so we'll need to do a skid landing. Just lean back on me,' he shouts in my ear. So we land sliding along the dewy grass, Dave breaking my fall. I unfasten myself from him and I'm whooping with joy, adrenaline and relief coursing through me. I turn to thank Dave for accompanying me on the descent and see he too is filled with joy and elation – it's his 250th jump, but he says it always gives him a buzz. I'm so high I'm not allowed to drive the car home.

I was grateful for Dave's accompaniment on my sky dive, as I'd never have dared do it on my own, but his reassuring presence gave me the courage to risk letting go. Too often we can feel trapped in a life that never fully satisfies, and I would suggest that good accompaniment can allow us to take the risks that can lead us to that sense of inner freedom I felt falling through the air. On my inner journey the way to this freedom has come through a learning to let go, a willingness to enter and stay in liminal space, and learning to live more in the moment. Significantly, any development in my spiritual life hasn't drawn me away from people into a protected bubble, but rather has impelled me into a deeper and fuller engagement with others and particularly those on the margins of our society.

LETTING GO OF FEAR

The image of rolling out of a plane stays with me today, when I think about letting go and discovering real freedom. Over the years, I've been learning the benefit of ceasing to cling to my own carefully constructed defences, ways of keeping people out and techniques of trying to avoid pain and personable vulnerability. These defences, at times, seem so firmly embedded, that it feels like a lifetime's work to dismantle them and choose a less certain but ultimately more life-giving way. Just as Dave the Marine came with me out of that plane, we need people we can trust to help us let go of all that holds us back. It's only really as I've reached my fifties and begun to seriously realise and believe that I'm going to die that I can begin to see the foolishness of pursuing the agenda of personal achievement, success and individual autonomy.

Returning to the description of Max clinging on to the gatepost at the beginning of the book, that scene is a metaphor for how in the West we cling to our sense of immortality. I would suggest that because we fear death and refuse to explore our fear of not being here any more, we become obsessed with defending our life at all costs and fill our lives with distractions. Paradoxically, it means that, for many, the one life that we so value isn't truly savoured and enjoyed but becomes a thing to defend at all costs and a focus for constant anxiety. When all our energy goes into clinging, then the sheer exhilaration and joy of the journey can be lost. Old age in our culture becomes something to fear, and looking old, which of course reminds us of the natural decay of our bodies, becomes something to be avoided. People invest heavily in skin care to remove and hide wrinkles, hair is dyed, extra vitamins are taken in an attempt to slow down the ageing process, great care is taken over clothing to make us look younger. One of the reasons the National Health Service in Britain is in financial crisis is because of the increasing amounts spent on keeping frail and vulnerable elderly people alive by spending more on life-prolonging treatment.

I was once visiting someone at home who'd had a recent heart attack and was close to death, and I was with him as he had a further massive heart attack. Paramedics were called, but the man died some minutes before they arrived. I told them it was too late, but because the deceased hadn't signed a letter asking not to be resuscitated, they insisted on attaching the wires of a defibrillator to him and shocking his dead body for another 15 minutes, which was hugely distressing for his family and seemed an affront to the dead man's dignity. The paramedics were severely embarrassed and apologetic, but that's what the rules of their job stated they had to do. As they left, calm was restored. I said some ancient, well-worn prayers and anointed his body with oil, and the gathered family were able to begin to say their goodbyes.

The forced attempt to revive people seems symptomatic of our society's refusal to accept death as a natural and inevitable end to life. Benjamin Franklin once famously asserted that 'nothing can be said to be certain, except death and taxes', and just as some people and hugely wealthy corporations seek to avoid paying tax, so many of us want to avoid thinking about death. In Victorian times, sex was the great taboo, but death was on full and extravagant display; today, this has been reversed: sex is openly talked about, but death has become hidden from view. This denial and fear of death, I think, is at the heart of much of the negative individualism and alienation so prevalent in society. If we see life as something to cling on to, if we have to protect ourselves from the threat of disease, protect our territory from those who might damage it or diminish our securely created world, then that inevitably leads to a culture of fear and suspicion. If my security is based on the value of my property, then of course I'm going to be angry with anyone who plans to open a wind farm down the road which might cause my house price to diminish. If, above all, I want to cling on to this one life of mine, then I'll need to learn to compete with others and glory in personal achievement and the amassing of possessions. The accumulation of wealth and the countless possibilities for distraction that abound in our technological age are a comfort and welcome distraction from that deeply buried but still potent fear of nothingness. Zen master Julian Daizan Skinner challenges this way of thinking: 'Intrinsic to this world view is a sense that I am insignificant and vulnerable in this hostile universe and that sooner or later I will be destroyed. Life is a battle for existence' (Skinner 2017, p.103).

The refreshing thing for me, living in the bush in Uganda, was that most people had so little, they were unencumbered by those sorts of fears. Pusi told me the story of how cattle raiders came to his mud hut in the middle of the night. They pushed through the door and pointed a gun at his head as he was sleeping on the floor next to his wife. He woke up, looked at them and laughed and told them he had nothing worth stealing. 'Look, you can either shoot me or go, I don't care which, I'm going back to sleep now,' and with that he put his head back under the covers. He said he waited, then heard them shuffle off and awoke the next day grateful to be alive and enjoyed the walk to the borehole to pump water more than ever. Pusi himself had once been a cattle raider and laughed at the irony of them trying to steal from him, but he'd given up that life long ago and through his letting go of the machismo and greed of that life had found a new freedom. He was a great accompanier, because he loved his life but wasn't clinging on to it, and was able to enjoy each day and the people he encountered with a rare freedom, just like that freedom I'd felt floating through the air before my parachute opened.

In my mud hut in Uganda I used to wake at 2 a.m. every night, as the rats came alive in the grass roof. Unable to get back to sleep, I'd examine my list of fears: being chewed by a rat, bitten by a snake, getting malaria, breaking my leg hours from the nearest hospital, kidnapped by cattle raiders. Once, I thought I heard people gathering outside my flimsy door, only to listen more intently and work out that a pig had knocked over my jerry-can of water and was drinking from it. At first, I felt paralysed by fear, but slowly learnt to manage it. I began to see this night vigil as an opportunity to confront my fears, so I lay there grasping a smooth wooden 'holding cross', not even able to pray with words, but just noticing my fears, staying with them, going through the list and just breathing gently through them. Then I'd get up in the deep darkness of the hut, open the door and look up to the immense starlit sky, walk round the back of the hut and urinate. It became a kind of ritual, this night-time pissing symbolising the release and letting go of fear; then I'd get back into bed and quickly slip into sleep.

Soon after I started working with Travellers, I woke from a dream with the words 'Will they like me?' fresh on my lips, feeling again full of fear. 'What was that about?' I thought, and quickly realised it was my anxiety about my new role and how I'd be able to relate to the Travellers and Gypsies I was beginning to meet. The question 'Will they like me?', though, is a question we can spend our lives worrying about – the fear of what people think about us.

The answer to my 'Will they like me?' question came, of course, when I began to get out and about and meet Travellers. The fear was there initially, but as soon as I made contact and engaged with people my fears began to dissipate. As I become more secure in my role, I see my task as building trust and respect amongst the community rather than needing to be liked. In fact, the more I've stopped worrying about and let go of the need to be liked, the more I've been blessed with many growing friendships. Accompaniment is like that – the less you try to do it and the less you try to get results from it the more it bears fruit.

At the heart of all the great world religions is this call to let go of this clinging on to selfish individualism and personal security. In Buddhism, there's the call to detach ourselves from our cravings and desires, best summed up in the word 'nekkhama'. Hinduism calls this 'sannyasa'. In Islam, it is best translated as submission to Allah who alone possesses all power. In the Christian Gospels, Jesus teaches that only when we are prepared to lose our life will we find it. 'Very truly, I tell you, unless a grain of wheat falls into the earth and dies, it remains just a single grain; but if it dies, it bears much fruit' (John 12:24).

The Charter for Compassion, inspired by Karen Armstrong, declares: 'Compassion impels us to work tirelessly to alleviate the suffering of our fellow creatures, to dethrone ourselves from the centre of our world and put another there' (Charter for Compassion 2019). Maybe it's only when we learn to 'dethrone ourselves from the centre of our world' that true compassion, freedom, peace and mutuality can grow. It's when we stop protecting our imagined kingdoms and seeing others as threats that we begin to find a new security based on our common humanity, learning to love life and not cling to it. This notion of learning to let go, in order to embrace a greater freedom, is beautifully summed up in words from the *Tao Te Ching* (Palmer 1993, p.86):

> *Learn to yield and be soft*
> *If you want to survive*
> *Learn to bow*
> *And you will stand to your full height*
> *Learn to empty yourself*
> *And be filled by the Tao*
> *The way a valley empties itself into a river*
> *Use up all you are*
> *And then you will be made new*
> *Learn to have nothing*
> *And you will have everything.*

To accompany others well, I'm learning that I need to let go of the fears that get in the way of being more fully open to my true self and others. The more I let go of my need to be in control, to prove myself to others, even to be good and helpful, the better I'll be able to accompany others. We're much less likely to impose our own fears and prejudices on others if we feel more free of them ourselves.

This, perhaps, sounds great in principle, but how do we get to this place of freedom? I believe we're able to risk lowering our defences and entering a new kind of freedom by being prepared to inhabit what I described in Chapter 3 as liminal space.

LIMINAL SPACE

As a young enthusiastic vicar, determined to save the world and working hard to change my bit of it in North Walsall, I began to notice that some of the best work I did with people was on my day off. People would knock on the door to arrange a baptism or something else, I'd invite them in, and suddenly they'd begin to share all kinds of important stuff with me. The quality of my encounters with people when I was in my day-off mode and feeling a little out of role was somehow always better and more fulfilling. Slowly it began to dawn on me that my intense busyness and focus to be the best priest I possibly could were getting in the way of how I related to people. These days, if you ask people how they are, one of the commonest stock responses is 'busy', which seems like a fairly defensive reply that tells you little about how the person is and is designed to limit your conversation, knowing the person is 'busy'. I try now never to reply to enquiries about my wellbeing with 'I'm busy' but if I am, I say something like 'Life is very full,' which, hopefully, might open up the encounter further.

I've found that sitting down with someone is also more likely to open up a conversation than standing, ready to move on. The act of sitting down with someone is a way of inviting them into a space you are creating for each other, making time, not wasting time.

The expression to 'sit with something' suggests an openness to possibility and the other. Classically, the Buddha sitting under the Bodhi tree represents the ultimate abandonment of busyness and complete entry into liminal space, the not knowing, not striving, a place of emptying. Daizan Skinner talks about 'cultivating your guts', or 'hara', learning to sit with your feelings. This involves a breathing meditation, concentrating on your belly and lower abdomen, and helps people become more grounded and not so trapped in the intellect, which tends to compare and separate. He teaches that Hara meditation leads us away from a place of not knowing and into a place of intuitive wisdom: 'It is a place beyond dualities. Within this place you can know for yourself, without a shadow of doubt, that you are not separate' (Skinner 2017).

Hara meditation also helps us integrate negative emotions, which we usually deal with by either seeking to suppress them or act out of them, neither of which is helpful. Instead, he suggests we learn to sit with and create a space for these feelings to come and go. They're not repressed or allowed to create havoc but simply observed. By creating space, fears and negative emotions can lose their hold on us. As I sat with my grief and anger over the treatment of little Emir, mentioned in Chapter 6, I eventually found a sense of peace and new purpose. Having the courage to stay with and accompany our difficult feelings can be transformative. This, in turn, will provide us with the resources not to flinch from being with others *in extremis*.

I was asked by Sally, who was in recovery from alcohol addiction, to help her say farewell to three elderly and increasingly sick horses she'd been looking after for a number of years. It was a cold February day when we met at the stables. The horses where on top of Windswept Hill and we walked up with the vet and his bag full of syringes and barbiturates. I asked him how much time he had, and he replied he was in no hurry and it would take as long as we needed it to. He began by giving each horse a hefty sedative, which calmed them down, then the first horse was led over with a rope by Sally. Sally read out a well-crafted prayer of thanks for all the love and constancy the horse had given her and, as the vet loaded his syringe, I took out a pot of oil and anointed the huge forehead with the sign of the cross, held the horse's neck and whispered a blessing in its ear. I held the rope as the injection went in, guiding the horse down with a great thud, as in seconds the drug paralysed its nervous system. Sally knelt down beside the horse as it sighed and snorted its last breaths, saying her farewells. It was gut-wrenchingly awful. When humans die, the grief takes weeks, months to come out, somehow we're defended from the full crushing force of death which would be unbearable, but with animals it just feels immediate. All I could think as I stood there was, 'I don't want to be here, I can't stand this. I need a drink. If I'm feeling this, my God, what must Sally be feeling?' I knew, though, that I had to stay and that somehow inhabiting this place of extreme discomfort, this place between life and death, was at the heart of what it means to be in relationship with one another and all sentient beings.

We covered the dead horse. By this time we were all shaking with the cold and emotion. The next one came along and the rituals were slowly repeated, and then the third. Finally, it was over and we went for tea as the knacker man moved in to dispose of the corpses. I felt bleak, empty, useless standing there. I wanted to flee, but knew I had to be with Sally in that place. She could have just got the knacker man to shoot the horses, but choosing to be with them as they died she knew to be a hugely significant part of a process to help her move on.

The best and worst of being a priest is being present with people at liminal times such as birth, marriage and death, and somehow trying to help them reflect on the transitions they are going through. Increasingly, I think I want to assist people not in managing their grief, fear or joy but rather learning to stay with it and eventually integrating it into the person they're becoming. As I managed to stay with my feelings of acute discomfort as the horses died, as I managed to stay with Sally's intense grief, so I was able to integrate some of my own feelings of grief and loss by just staying in that empty place. There wasn't anything to say – any words of comfort would have seemed trite – but being prepared to stay with Sally in that bleak place was vital.

I find that in the chaplaincy work that I do with Gypsies and Travellers the ability to stay in what can feel an uncomfortable space rather than just quickly move on is vital to the way I work. For very good reasons, Travellers are suspicious of outsiders, following centuries of persecution and present-day discrimination, so when I turn up on a Traveller site for the first time, I have to hold this in mind. I'll wear my dog collar to identify myself as a religious person rather than someone in authority from the council or police, and slowly move around the site. The first fear I have to overcome is that of being bitten by the inevitable yapping dogs, but my greatest fear is of feeling useless, not being able to offer anything. In a sense, I don't have much to offer, only myself; people's initial indifference could be taken personally and the temptation is often to move on quickly or only visit the people I know. I find, though, if I have the will just to stand about feeling useless, I'll often fall into conversation and out of that, relationships slowly grow. Learning not to fear emptiness, but rather seeing it as creating space for the other is, to me, a crucial part of accompaniment.

Philosopher, sociologist, teacher and political activist Simone Weil (1959, p.66) describes entering this state of emptiness as vital to learning: 'Attention consists of suspending our thought, leaving it detached, empty, and ready to be penetrated by the object...above all our thought should be empty, waiting, not seeking anything, but ready to receive in its naked truth the object which is to penetrate it.' For Simone Weil, we learn by paying attention through emptying ourselves, learning to wait without our expectations getting in the way. So too in accompaniment, creating space to give full attention to the other is crucial.

At the beginning of the fourth century, partly out of protest at a church gone soft and institutionalised, as Christianity became the state religion under Emperor Constantine, men and women began to retreat to the vast spaces of the Egyptian desert and became known as the Desert Mothers and Fathers. The desert became the liminal space, where, in solitude, they could encounter God and work towards what they called purity of heart. One of their catchphrases was 'Go and sit in your cell, and your cell will teach you everything.' It's that wisdom again that if we learn to sit with ourselves and risk solitude, then we'll find a greater sense of belonging to everyone and everything. In the fourth century, people would travel from the cities to meet these holy men and women living in the desert, which symbolised liminal space. They would come and ask for just a word of wisdom to take back with them, and the stories of these seekers of truth became known throughout the Mediterranean world. Mother Amma Syncletica advised seekers to learn to stay in one place in order to grow spiritually:

> If you find yourself in a monastery do not go to another place, for that will harm you a great deal. Just as the bird who abandons the eggs she was sitting on, prevents them from hatching, so the monk or the nun grows cold and their faith dies when they go from place to place. (Ward 1984, Sayings 6)

In Judaism and Islam, the liminal space of the desert or the mountain is also the place of encounter with and revelation from God. In Hinduism and Buddhism, it is the mountain or the forest. Wild, untamed and empty places seem to be where individuals can go to find the necessary space to encounter God or their true selves. Making space for myself, learning to be comfortable in silence, with just my faithful companion, my breath, all seem to be ways that increase my desire to make room and time for others. So when I'm accompanying others, I'm learning that I don't need to worry about gaps or pauses, and rush to fill them with words, but rather wait, get out of the way and let the other fill that space.

A few years ago, I was asked to do a wedding blessing/celebration by two friends, one of whom was a Buddhist, and I asked him what wisdom he could give me from his faith tradition to put in the ceremony. He said, 'Maybe something like "nothing lasts forever".' I looked at him, smiled, and said, 'Do you think that's really appropriate for a wedding? Aren't you going to be pledging to be together for life? It'll sound like you're building in a pre-nuptial agreement just in case things go wrong!' I went away and thought about what he'd said and then it began to make sense. If nothing lasts forever, then we need to learn to live more fully in the moment and deeply cherish one another, which is probably the essence of deeply loving relationships. He also said that learning to be empty and being free from possessiveness were at the heart of his spiritual practice, which involved a lot of sitting in silence. So we decided that part of the wedding ritual, which was to take place in woodland, would be for the wedding guests to surround the couple in a circle, call down a blessing on them and have five minutes of silence. It was a profoundly countercultural moment for the hundred or so men, women and children gathered together, doing nothing, saying nothing, just being empty. All we could hear was the wind in the trees and one another breathing, staying in the moment.

'Don't just stand there, do something!' seems to be the mantra of Western society, which leads to so much stress, ill health and constant anxiety. We have become so used to constantly being on the move and busying ourselves that the thought of doing nothing feels deeply threatening, so rather than rest, reflect, or sit with our pain or joy, we seek to fill our leisure time with activity. This, of course, never fully satisfies, so we look for the next thing to fill the emptiness. I'm slowly learning that if, rather than avoiding and fearing emptiness, I enter it and stay with it, my life begins to feel more integrated and whole. If I learn to stay on the threshold a little longer, when I do cross it and step out into the world, I do so with much more purpose, energy and joy.

It took me five years to learn this wisdom after leaving the Pilsdon Community, whilst seeking what to do next with my life. I'd given myself a year off, thinking that would be time enough for me to enter the next phase of my life and to find the right job. Nothing came my way for the first or second year I was in exile at Hilfield Friary, but I kept myself busy, laying concrete, fixing roofs, gardening, cooking and cleaning. I then went to Uganda to explore my vocation as a peacemaker, but it didn't feel right long term. I applied for a couple of jobs in churches on run-down council estates but didn't even get an interview. It was now five years since I left Pilsdon, and I began to despair about how my life seemed to lack any overall purpose or direction. Here I was with loads of experience but no job and no future. I then made the conscious decision to give up looking for the next step and try and live purely in the moment. In the small chapel at Pilsdon was the hub of an ancient cartwheel, which sat in the centre of the room with a small candle burning in it. I'd always loved the image of the centre of the wheel being still, whilst everything turned around it – what T. S. Eliot called 'the still point of the turning world' – and I decided to try and live as though I was at that still point. I resolved to give up on searching or even waiting for the next thing and just be. In my spiritual practice I gave up any words or actions, just sitting in silence and breathing. Twice a day I spent 30 minutes doing nothing, expecting nothing, trying to be empty, being at the hub of the wheel. As the *Tao Te Ching* reminds us:

> *Thirty spokes on a cartwheel*
> *Go towards the hub that is the centre*
> *But look there is nothing at the centre*
> *And that is precisely why it works*
> *In a house or a room, it is the empty space*
> *The doors the windows that make it useable*

Palmer (1993, p.46)

Of course, once I'd entered that liminal space and given up on the regrets of the past and anxiety about the future, my life began to take shape. I was offered a job working with Travellers and Gypsies, decided to write a book and was given the opportunity to go to the Solomon Islands for three months. It was when I was able to give up ambition for the future and surrender to living in the moment that finally things began to shift for me. Learning to be at the still point at the hub of the wheel allowed me to finally find my way and pick up a renewed sense of energy as the wheel of the future direction of my life began to turn.

Crucial to the art of accompaniment for me has been a willingness to enter that space of not knowing, being prepared to be empty in order not to get in the way of being open to the other. To create that space to allow another person to be fully themselves, without imposing our inner noise on them, is a great gift. Gerry Hughes, Jesuit and author, when training people in spiritual accompaniment often used the phrase 'We train people not to do damage to others, the rest we leave to the Holy Spirit.' I've always taken that to mean that we need to be aware of imposing our stuff consciously or unconsciously on others. It's the opposite of fundamentalism, which seeks to fill people's minds with a rigidly constructed world view. I increasingly distrust people who preach certainty, particularly when it begins to exclude others. I think deeper truth is encountered when we're prepared to enter that place of emptiness, not knowing, as rather than close down space it creates space for the other.

LIVING IN THE MOMENT

The story is told of some seekers after truth who asked the Buddha who he was. Some asked if he was a guru. 'No,' he replied. Others asked if he was a prophet. 'No,' he replied. Still others asked if he was a healer. 'No,' he replied. 'Well who are you then?' they asked.

'I am one who is awake,' he answered.

To be awake, to live in the present moment seems to be at the heart of most spiritual practices. In Buddhist practice, paying attention to each breath is a way of learning to stay in the moment. In the yogic traditions of Hinduism, again, staying with the breathing and concentrating on the body's movement keeps the devotee in the eternal moment. In Islam too, the salat prayer postures and words focus the believer on Allah alone. In the Christian contemplative tradition, there are numerous techniques for staying in the moment, again through focusing attention on the body, breathing exercises or the repetition of a mantra.

On my own journey, the people who've most impressed me have been those who seem to live in the moment. People who have a capacity to see things as they really are, unencumbered by fear about the future or trapped in the past. Most of the Romany Gypsies I know very much live in the moment, which, I think, comes from their recent nomadic past. If you're regularly moving on, then there's no time to get too invested in plans for the future, and the past is literally behind you. I know now that if I want to visit Travellers, there's little point in arranging things too far in advance, as plans can change depending on what the day brings, so I've learnt just to ring and say I'm on my way. When you live day by day and in the moment, a diary doesn't really work. The beauty for me of this way of being is that when you're with people, that's the focus and nothing else, and you can feel really met.

Too often, I meet people who are really somewhere else, still caught up in their last meeting or keen to move on to the next challenge, and, yes, I also allow myself to be dragged away from being fully awake to another. As someone who loves multitasking and doing several jobs at a time, juggling various commitments, it's easy not to stay in the moment and not give the person in front of you your full attention. I'll never forget Peter, a man with Asperger's syndrome, telling me, 'Jonathan, you need to learn to just do one thing at a time.' That was the only way he could cope with what, for him, were the otherwise impossible multiple pressures to relate to too many things and people at once, and staying in the moment doing one thing at a time is wisdom for us all. Tich Nat Han, Vietnamese Buddhist monk and peacemaker, famously says, 'When you're doing the washing up, do the washing up.' I'm slowly learning that if I concentrate on doing just one thing at a time, the day is still full of variety, things still get done, and somehow the day seems to flow more freely. I recognise also when someone is giving me their full attention, focusing solely on the person in front of them, and what a gift it is. I can also clearly tell when I'm not living in the moment and that usually coincides with stress or tiredness or both together. I find myself jumping from one thing to another, not managing to finish anything, feeling twitchy, out of sorts, everything feeling more difficult than usual. My temptation is to work harder, push myself on, achieve something, but that, I know, to be a trap that I too readily fall into. Worse still is to go and do something to make me feel better temporarily, eat something, have a coffee to stimulate me even more, have a few drinks at the end of the day to make myself feel better. All these strategies, in the end, are avoidance and likely to become addictive. What I'm learning is to stay in the moment and look at what is really troubling me, to wake up to my compulsions and fears, and not fight or supress them, but feel them and let them pass.

What I know helps me stay in the moment, aside from some meditative practices, are two things: walking in nature and focusing my attention on making something. There's an hour-long circular walk around the Friary which, if I go at a meditative pace, takes an hour and a half. Going at that pace might not burn off many calories or be part of a physical fitness regime but, just like Satish Kumar, who walks for an hour every day, I always feel better for it and re-balanced by it, paying attention to the rhythm of my walking, looking at and listening to the life around me. Working with my hands also seems to return me to the moment. If I'm knocking nails into tiles on a roof, my focus is solely on that. People talk about 'losing' themselves in creating a bit of art or craft, but I would say every time I make a basket, I find myself.

We have a monthly craft workshop at the friary which is open to all and led by a particularly extrovert, bumptious and irreverent woman, which starts off fairly raucous and full of laughter, but as it gets deeper into the day, it invariably progresses into silence, as the men and women, through the focus on their particular craft, are led into the moment.

A danger of this staying in the moment, mindfulness and spirituality in general, is that it can lead to an even greater sense of individualism and just become another tool for personal advancement. Certainly mindfulness is being adopted by business as a way of improving performance and enhancing productivity. Peter Tyler worries that the preponderance of online courses and apps in mindfulness are leading to a privatisation of spirituality. As he writes:

> Slavoj Žižek, the pungent Slovenian critic, describes it as ideally suited to the needs of the late capitalist world when he states: 'the "Western Buddhist" meditative stance is arguably the most effective way for us to fully participate in capitalist dynamics whilst retaining the semblance of mental health'. (Tyler 2018, p.66)

If, through practising mindfulness, we seek to shore up our defences and cope with the pressures of life, then there's the danger that we subtly become trapped once more in the narrative of individual achievement, which leads to separation and exclusion. For spiritual practice to have any integrity, it must lead us into relationships with others and not just the people we like or feel comfortable around. Being fully present to ourselves will lead us to being more present with others. I know that seeking solitude and retreating at times from others paradoxically allow me to feel more connected to people and better accompany them.

I spent 30 days on a silent retreat in North Wales, and midway through my time, wandered into the nearby town of Rhyl, full of holidaymakers from the poorer parts of Merseyside and the West Midlands. Standing in the streets of this unremarkable, grey, windswept seaside town, I felt myself utterly overcome with a deep sense of love for all the people around me. I felt completely connected to them, as though I was seeing people for the first time as they really are – they and I were one, there were no others. Later, on that same retreat, I had a similar experience swimming alone one morning in the sea, looking back at the mountains of Snowdonia, feeling completely at one with the landscape, that same feeling that everything belongs. It seemed that the deeper I'd gone into exploring my inner life, the stronger my connection with everyone and everything else. Learning to be in the moment had led to learning to be with others.

BEING WITH

If one of the benefits of developing our inner life is to have a growing sense of spaciousness, which all the mystical traditions point to, then it necessarily follows that we will have more room for others. Theresa of Avila, a sixteenth-century Spanish mystic, talked about the dilation of the heart, literally the expansion of the heart, and developing this inner sense of expansiveness, which then leads to a generosity towards others, which is something our society urgently needs. The illusion of individuality that fuels consumerism, leads to violence, hatred and disdain, and to so much isolation can best be challenged by a spirituality that promotes a sense of belonging. Self-sufficiency and personal autonomy can only be fully dethroned by a way of being that puts being with others at its heart. If our fundamental human problem is isolation, then the answer won't be found in laboratories, in ever more sophisticated artificial intelligence or medicine at the frontiers of knowledge, but rather in our reclaiming what we already have, that sense of belonging together. Too much of Western religion, and the way Eastern traditions are interpreted so often in the West, places the individual at the centre. Fundamentalism grows in Islam when Sharia is placed before the Umma, in Buddhism when the Dharma comes before the Sangha and in Christianity when the inerrancy of scripture and the rule-governed behaviour that follows it come before the beloved community.

In movements for social and environmental justice, the focus on single issues at the expense of a more rounded and deeply rooted base can lead to fractures in the movement and the rapid burnout of activists. What has the potential to resource people and hold them together, aside from a common vision, is the ability to develop a deep sense of belonging to one another and the earth. The years I've spent living in the two very earthy but prayerful communities of Hilfield and Pilsdon have convinced me of the importance of working hard to create safe places where people can belong together. Part of the work of building community is taking time to resource individuals. In my mentoring of people over the years, I always like to ask the question 'What resources you?' or, put another way, 'What gives you life?' and then encourage people to build that into their daily living. My experience is that, when a person feels well resourced on an inner level, this, in turn, leads them to share this joy in their interaction with others and strengthens community.

Being at peace with ourselves has to be the starting point for being well with others. When we overcome the otherness in ourselves, when we befriend our shadow, make peace with what we hate in ourselves, then our sense of belonging to others inevitably grows. My sense of being at one with myself is what allows me to be at one with others, and indeed reach out of my comfort zone to include others. This allows me to risk being vulnerable and take up a more nuanced and less polarised view of the world. The great lie that is taught to so many of us from a young age is that we are separate, autonomous beings and we need to find a strong independent identity, which we must defend at all costs. I think a better, and definitely more life-giving narrative is that we are people who are called to live together and our security comes not from what we possess but rather the depth and connection of our relationships with others. Accompaniment can be the tool that helps us to realise we belong together.

This more positive world view is vital if we are to challenge the narrative of austerity and immigration policy in Britain since 2010, which has been that resources are scarce and we need to fear those who are a potential drain on resources – the poor, disabled, those in the criminal justice system and immigrants. The closure of children's centres and youth services and the demonising of immigrants have led to a rise in poverty, crime and prejudice and growing fear and insecurity, which, in turn, have led to more isolation, exclusion and loneliness.

One of my first jobs as chaplain to Travellers was to accompany a young Irish Traveller woman and her mother and aunt to a family court hearing to try to regain custody of her child. The family were completely out of their depth in this alien environment, as were the judge, social workers and legal teams who, it became clear, had no understanding of Traveller culture. For the Travellers, who had low levels of literacy, the very formal surroundings and stress on documents and the written word were deeply intimidating. The court officials, likewise, had no background in the culture the family belonged to. Their focus was solely on the suitability of the 17-year-old mother to bring up the child, completely ignorant of the way children in the Traveller community are brought up by aunties, uncles and grandparents in large extended families. I wasn't allowed to speak in court and felt a growing sense of frustration as this disconnect continued through the proceedings. The court's final decision was that the child should remain in care.

If only the social worker giving the report had been able to just go and spend time with the family over a number of visits, just be with them and build trust and relationships, I think her report would have been quite different. But she was ruled by that narrative again: resources and time are scarce. I had the luxury of being able to sit with the family and get to know them whilst waiting for the court to be free, in adjournment time, and over a couple of lunch breaks. I had the space and was able to make the time to begin to build trust with them. I went away from the court feeling frustrated but also convinced that my method of seeking to accompany people, just being with them, was how I wanted to frame my 'work' with Travellers. Yet even before this, for this model to work, I'd have to spend time just being with myself. I realised that if I was going to be any good at learning to be with others, I had to be totally comfortable in my own skin. This seemed to go back to the practice of doing nothing, learning to be comfortable just sitting, breathing, staying in the moment, creating an inner sense of spaciousness. Call it meditation, contemplation, living in the moment, being still, self-emptying or what you will, I've learnt that when I build this into my day, it paradoxically turns me outwards and makes me want to build relationships with others. If I feel tired, anxious or stressed, I know I'm going to struggle to build trust and friendship with anyone else and be comfortable doing nothing, just being with.

My mentor Graham Chadwick used to say to me that 'Contemplation is taking a long loving look at what is real.' I think the attempt to live in what Eckhart Tolle, writer and spiritual teacher, calls the 'power of now' (2001), what I would call the joy of the present moment, allows us to take a long loving look at the natural world with a growing sense of being an integral part of it and see others no longer as strangers or threats but people we belong with. The spirituality I want to practise isn't a fleeing from the world and all its grief and challenges, but rather something that seeks to look at what is good, what is difficult, sit with it, be with it, let it go, and be transformed by it. Any journey inwards is only of value if it then leads to real engagement and sense of belonging with others. The great gift of accompaniment is that it teaches us to enjoy people and nature for their own sake and not as a means to an end. Learning to be attentive to myself, to others and the natural world has led me into a deep and expanding sense of belonging to others and knowing the planet as my common and shared home. The fruit of this way of being with has led me into a deepening sense of joy and freedom.

EVERYTHING BELONGS

Halfway through my pilgrimage to Santiago de Compostela, I began to feel quite drained. I'd been a couple of days without really relating to anyone, my body was creaking a bit from walking 20 miles or so a day; I was in that dangerous place that a friend in Alcoholics Anonymous uses the acronym HALT to describe – hungry, angry, lonely, tired. All along the pilgrimage route were fountains where you could fill up with water, which would keep you going till the next watering place. That afternoon, I stopped at a fountain right on the edge of a town I'd walked through only to find it was dry, and I'd either have to continue for five miles over a sun-baked escarpment or go a mile back into town. I raised my pilgrim staff and hammered it into the ground with a volley of expletives, then looked around ashamedly to see if anyone was watching – fortunately not. I decided to go on without water through the heat of the afternoon, continuing to mutter a rich range of expletives. Eventually I got over the hill and as the sun slipped lower in the sky, it lit up the honey-coloured stone of the church of St Nicholas where I'd been told you could sleep the night. Outside, on a bench sat two men who smiled at me and beckoned me forward. They were drinking from white plastic cups and asked, 'Vino?'

'Si!' I replied, and I sat with them sipping fine wine from Genoa, where they explained they were from. They told me they were part of a pilgrim association spending two weeks offering hospitality. I sat with them watching other pilgrims pass. Two French cyclists turned up asking to stay but they were sent on their way. A young extrovert Hungarian woman asked whether there was room for her, and she was invited to continue walking; a scruffy young French-Canadian couple, carrying a tent, were invited to stay, two strapping German lads were directed to the next refuge and then a lone Italian cyclist was persuaded to form the last of our quartet. I took a shower round the back of the church and, as I was putting on a pair of woolly socks, I was told to leave my feet bare and summoned to the front of the eleventh-century Romanesque church. Vittorio and Paulo, our hosts, then donned short black woollen capes decorated with scallop shells, and I understood we were going to do a bit of religion. They read some prayers in Latin, then knelt at our feet, placed them in a bowl of warm water, gently washed them, tenderly dried them, and finally kissed them. Then it was time for supper, and we moved to a temporary trestle table in the middle of the church.

We had a starter of Italian cheese or prosciutto accompanied by more red wine from Genoa. Then it was time for the main course, pasta with pesto from Genoese basil, and I rather rudely asked for more, thinking that was it. Then the fish came, accompanied by a Genoese white wine, followed by the main course and back to 'vino tinto'. I grinned at the French-Canadian couple and said, 'This is just like Babette's Feast.' They nodded back vigorously, also feeling resonances with that film, where Babette serves a sumptuous feast to a whole village of strict Calvinist protestants, who survive on a miserable everyday diet of fish and bread soup. Fine pastries made by Italian nuns living up the road, stuffed with cream, were offered, then a final course of cheeses, followed by coffee, then grappa from a large bottle with a lemon inside. Before staggering to my bed at the back of the church, I asked what time we had to leave. I was told not to worry, that we'd be woken by 'dulce music'. Sure enough, whilst it was still dark, I was woken by a beautiful gentle aria from Puccini and quickly dressed. I didn't want the magical spell that had been woven the night before to be broken so tried to slip away unnoticed into the dark starlit morning, but Vittorio asked me to wait a moment, donned his cloak again and took me into the porch where he incanted a prayer of blessing and kissed me on both cheeks. I can still today feel the stubble on his face brushing against mine. My eyes filled with tears of joy and I walked out into the starlit morning feeling completely restored and full of energy. It was two hours before I stopped singing.

Appendix 1

Hints for Accompaniment

1. Take your time, don't enter into it expecting results or instant gratification; accompaniment doesn't work if you try to force it.
2. Don't be afraid of silence, pausing, waiting, or if nothing seems to be happening in the encounter; it might just be that what's being created is space for the other person.
3. Try not to let your own anxieties get in the way of the other person. Give them the space to be them, let their story unfold, don't try and impose your story on them.
4. Be prepared to stay with another person's difficult feelings and with your own. Don't get caught up in the emotion of your own feelings; notice them, stay with them, feel them, don't be led by them.
5. Enjoy the encounter with another person; encounter with another person can be a wonderful gift.
6. Learn to look with compassion on the other and learn to take a long loving look at people and the natural world.
7. Remember that accompaniment can occur in a variety of situations: working together, going for a walk, doing art together.
8. Sometimes you might need to change the frame. 'Have you thought about looking at things this way?'

9. Check that it feels like a fairly mutual process, and that you're not creating dependence.
10. Take time to reflect on your encounters. What gave life? What got in the way of our communication? What can I learn?

Appendix 2

Essential Ingredients for Living in Community

As social animals, living in community is how we are meant to be. We might live in an intentional community, a residential community or a neighbourhood, or be part of a community that gathers together regularly. These apply to all kinds of communities.

1. *Vision* is all-important as it's what gives purpose and binds a community together. It's a place to return to in times of difficulty and uncertainty, to strengthen commitment.
2. *Boundaries* give structure, rhythm and definition to a community, allow people to feel safe and also allow the community to exclude those who threaten its stability.
3. *Generosity* is a vital ingredient that encourages listening to one another and openness, and allows people to take risks and make mistakes without fearing judgement.
4. *Trust* builds the community relationship by relationship, and builds confidence and resilience.
5. *Need*: reaching out to those in need gives a community a purpose, and harnesses goodwill. Knowing our own needs helps us to live sustainably. Learning to depend on others strengthens community.
6. *Celebration* is vital to defining and binding a community together. Meal times are a daily celebration of community

life. Having an annual cycle of community celebrations helps bind people together. Spontaneity is good too!

References

Armstrong, R. J., Hellmann, J. W. and Short, W. J. (1999) *Francis of Assisi: Early Documents.* Vol. 3, *The Prophet.* New York: New City Press.

Austin Zen Center (2019) *Work Practice.* Austin, TX: Austin Zen Center. Accessed on 5 September 2018 at https://austinzencenter.org/work-practice

Berry, W. (1999) *The Selected Poems of Wendell Berry.* Washington, DC: Counterpoint.

Blake, W. (1972) *Complete Writings,* edited by G. Keynes. Oxford: Oxford University Press.

Bolton, M. (2012) *Loneliness – The State We're In.* Oxford: Age UK. Accessed on 7 June 2019 at www.campaigntoendloneliness.org/wp-content/uploads/Loneliness-The-State-Were-In.pdf

Cantacuzino, M. (2015) *The Forgiveness Project: Stories For a Vengeful Age.* London: Jessica Kingsley Publishers.

Chakrabortty, A. (2017) 'A civilised society supports people in need, but our brutal system shatters lives.' *The Guardian,* 6 December. Accessed on 2 March 2018 at www.theguardian.com/commentisfree/2017/dec/06/a-civilised-society-supports-people-in-need-but-our-brutal-system-shatters-lives

Charter for Compassion (2019) Charter for Compassion. Washington, DC: Citizens for Global Solutions. Accessed on 28 January 2019 at https://globalsolutions.org/charter-for-compassion

CHIPS (n.d.) What We Do. Accessed on 14 June 2019 at https://chipspeace.org/what-we-do

Cox, D. T., Shanahan, D. F., Hudson, H. L., Plummer, K. E., Siriwardena, G. M., Fuller, R. A., et al. (2017) Doses of neighborhood nature: The benefits for mental health of living with nature. *BioScience, 67*(2), 147–155. Accessed on 15 June at https://academic.oup.com/bioscience/article/67/2/147/2900179

Devlin, A. (2017) 'OUT! OUT! OUT!' Dramatic moment hundreds of angry locals including children confronted travellers who had moved into Weston-super-Mare park. *The Sun,* 21 August. Accessed on 23 August 2017 at www.thesun.co.uk/news/4285981/weston-super-mare-travellers-park-video

Dubord, M. (2016) Christmas Eve 2015 Sermon, by Rev. Michel Dubord. *Pine Gate Newsletter, 15*(1). Accessed on 27 March 2018 at https://pinegate.wordpress.com/2016/08/12/christmas-eve-2015-sermon-by-rev-michel-dubord

Eddo-Lodge, R. (2017) *Why I'm No Longer Talking to White People about Race.* London: Bloomsbury Publishing.

Eisenstein, C. (2013) *The More Beautiful World Our Hearts Know Is Possible.* Berkeley, CA: North Atlantic Books.

Eisenstein, C. (2018) *Climate: A New Story.* Berkeley, CA: North Atlantic Books.

Francis, Pope (2015) *On Care for Our Common Home: Laudato Si'.* Indiana, IN: Our Sunday Visitor.

Future Roots (2016) 'I Know They Know what People Say I Am' – C's Story. Future Roots. Accessed on 15 March 2018 at www.futureroots.net/i-know-what-people-say

Gerrard, N. (2017) 'How a simple plan to give dignity to dementia patients changed society.' *The Guardian,* 3 December. Accessed on 5 December 2017 at www.theguardian.com/commentisfree/2017/dec/03/johns-campaign-how-a-simple-plan-to-give-dignity-to-dementia-patients-changed-society

Guenther, Margaret (1992) *Holy Listening: Art of Spiritual Direction*. Lanham, MD: Rowman & Littlefield Publishers, Inc.

Jones, T. (2007) *Utopian Dreams*. London: Faber & Faber.

Jung, C. (1938) *Psychology and Religion: West and East*. Vol. 11, The Collected Works of CG Jung. New Haven: Yale University Press

Klein, N. (2016). Let them drown: The violence of othering in a warming world. *London Review of Books, 38*(11), 11–13. Accessed on 12 June 2019 at www.lrb.co.uk/v38/n11/naomi-klein/let-them-drown

Klein, N. (2017) *No Is Not Enough: Resisting Trump's Shock Politics and Winning the World We Need*. Chicago: Haymarket Books.

Kumar, S. (2016) My Life on the Move. Resurgence & Ecologist. Accessed on 18 March 2018 at www.resurgence.org/magazine/article4604-my-life-on-the-move.html

Le Bas, D. (2018) *The Stopping Places*. London: Penguin Books.

Mantle, J. (2000) *Britain's First Worker-Priests: Radical Ministry in a Post-War Setting*. London: SCM Press.

McCarthy, M. (2015) *The Moth Snowstorm: Nature and Joy*. London: John Murray.

McClauslen, J. (1998) *The Pilsdon Community, The First 40 Years 1958–1998*. Private circulation.

Monbiot, G. (2017a) How do we get out of this mess? *The Guardian*, 9 September. Accessed on 25 June 2019 at www.theguardian.com/books/2017/sep/09/george-monbiot-how-de-we-get-out-of-this-mess

Monbiot, G. (2017b) Public luxury for all or private luxury for some. *The Guardian*, 31 May. Accessed on 25 June 2019 at www.theguardian.com/commentisfree/2017/may/31/private-wealth-labour-common-space

Ó Tuama, P. (2013) *Sorrow for Your Troubles*. Norwich: Canterbury Press.

Office for National Statistics (2019) The cost of living alone. Accessed on 25 June 2019 at www.ons.gov.uk/peoplepopulationandcommunity/birthsdeathsandmarriages/families/articles/thecostoflivingalone/2019-04-04

Palmer, M. (1993) *Tao Te Ching: A New Translation*. Shaftsbury: Element.

Parry, G., Van Cleemput, P., Peters, J., Moore, J., *et al*. (2004) *The Health Status of Gypsies & Travellers in England: Report of Department of Health Inequalities in Health Research Initiative Project 121/7500*. Sheffield: University of Sheffield.

Perrin, H. (1965) *Priest and Worker: The Autobiography of Henri Perrin*. London: Macmillan.

Raworth, K. (2017) *Doughnut Economics: Seven Ways to Think Like a 21st Century Economist*. Vermont: Chelsea Green Publishing.

Salgado, P. (2017) Choose to be with others, and for others. *London Catholic Worker, 56*(Winter), 4–5. Accessed on 9 June 2019 at www.londoncatholicworker.org/Winter2017.pdf

Skinner, J. D. (2017) *Practical Zen: Meditation and Beyond*. London: Singing Dragon.

Smith, G. (1982) *Pilsdon Morning*. Bridport: Creeds.

Smith, P. (1962) *Letters from a Community*. Private circulation.

Tolle, E. (2001) *The Power of Now*. London: Hodder and Stoughton.

Transition Network (2016) Principles: The Values and Principles That Guide Us. Transition Network. Accessed on 4 April 2018 at https://transitionnetwork.org/about-the-movement/what-is-transition/principles-2

Tsu, L. (1989) *Tao Te Ching*. New York: Vintage.

Tyler, P. (2018) *Christian Mindfulness: Theology and Practice*. London: SCM Press.

Vanier, J. and Maigre, F. X. (2018) *A Cry Is Heard: My Path to Peace*. New London, CT: Twenty-Third Publications.

Voskoboynik, D. M. (2019) Confronting Extinction. Red Pepper. Accessed on 3 February 2018 at www.redpepper.org.uk/confronting-extinction

Ward, B. (1984) *The Sayings of the Desert Fathers*. Kalamazoo, MI: Cistercian Publications.

Warner, F. (2008) *Gentle Dying, A: The Simple Guide to Achieving a Peaceful Death*. London: Hay House Ltd.

Webster, M. (1997) *Community Arts Workers: Finding Voices, Making Choices: Creativity for Social Change*. Nottingham: Educational Heretics Press.

Weil, S. (1959) *Waiting for God* [letters and essays]. Oakville, OM: Capricorn Books.

Welch, J. (1982) *Spiritual Pilgrims: Carl Jung and Teresa of Avila*. New York: Paulist Press.

Williams, J. G. (1996) *The Girard Reader*. New York: Crossroad Publishing Company.

Wilshire, B. (1998) *Wild Hunger: The Primal Roots of Modern Addiction*. Lanham, MD: Rowman & Littlefield.